READING TOES

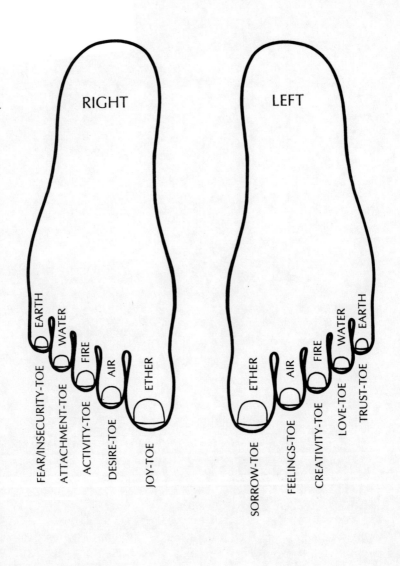

IMRE SOMOGYI

Reading Toes

YOUR FEET AS REFLECTIONS
OF YOUR PERSONALITY

Translated from the Dutch by
Robert Kamer

SAFFRON WALDEN
THE C.W. DANIEL COMPANY LIMITED

First published in The Netherlands
by Uitgeverij Fundament, Arnhem
under the title: *Tenen Lezen*

This English language edition was
first published in the United Kingdom in 1997
by The C.W. Daniel Company Limited
1 Church Path, Saffron Walden,
Essex, CB10 1JP, England

Copyright © Uitgeverij Fundament, Arnhem 1992 & 1997

Photographs: Ted Sluymer
Illustrations: Theo Akkerman

ISBN 0 85207 310 0

Produced in association with
Book Production Consultants plc
25–27 High Street, Chesterton, Cambridge CB4 1ND, England

Printed and bound in Great Britain by Biddles Ltd
King's Lynn, Norfolk

CONTENTS

Introduction

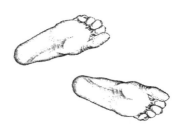

Toe-reading developed during a period when my wife Margriet and I decided it was time to work on ourselves. Both of us, Margriet by way of yoga, and I through alternative medicine, ended up in a small group of people who wanted to take a course in polarity therapy. What it would consist of we didn't really know, but we were told that it had everything to do with a balance of energy in the body. Polarity was described as acupuncture without needles but with the same effect.

In retrospect the effect may be the same, but the treatment itself is quite different. When given correctly, polarity therapy is far more painful than acupuncture. We found that to our cost, for our teacher told us: "You cannot apply a therapy if you yourself haven't undergone it in all its aspects. If not, you don't know what you're talking about." Thus we learned that foot reflex massage, which is a part of polarity therapy, can feel as if someone is working your feet with knives. We learned that, in the foot, reflexes of the whole body can be found. Someone with acute laryngitis has, according to the theory of foot reflex massage, a painful big toe.

Polarity therapy takes it a step further, and involves emotions. Sorrow, for instance, settles in the throat. As the clear proof of this, a woman, whose big toe was massaged gently, screamed at the top of her lungs, because of all the bottled-up sorrow. A sensitive left little toe, to take another example, reveals pessimism and often sexual problems.

Fascinated by this phenomenon we looked further for connections between emotions and pain in the foot. During our training, in which we students applied polarity massage to each other, we interviewed our fellow students extensively. We discovered that not only painful areas can tell us about emotions, but that the position and the shape of the toes relate to the way we deal with emotions too.

After this discovery we were so fascinated that we observed endless rows of bare feet on beaches, in swimming pools, in outdoor cafes and in saunas. We chuckled at someone with a mega macho appearance and irritating macho behaviour. His totally hidden left little toe told us that he obviously compensated for his sexual problems with his big biceps.

We were able to check our gradually developed theories at parties. Toe-reading acted as a good learning process. Reading toes at parties proved to have big advantages before having toe-reading sessions under other conditions. The reason is obvious: people in a happy mood are much more open than during a serious confrontation with a therapist. We gradually acquired a reputation for "having some interesting things to say". On every festive occasion there was someone who told others that we had such an interesting hobby. When people insisted, we performed our toe-reading act as 'entertainment'.

On an intercontinental flight I was consulted by the entire crew of the plane, after I had read the toes of a purser in a moment of frankness. On the flight back another crew turned out to have heard about this new way of 'head shrinking' (sometimes your reputation precedes you). A stewardess came up to me and checked if I was the same gentleman her colleagues had told her about. She invited me to have a drink in the pantry and to tell her something about the phenomenon of toe-reading because "…they had heard such extraordinary stories about it…" I didn't get much sleep on that flight, but I read toes from stewardess to captain, to everybody's satisfaction.

Be it at parties or under more serious circumstances, the toe-reading sessions had one thing in common: we were always asked about the origin of our knowledge. Every time we had to answer that our 'knowledge' had come from many places, and that we had combined the experiences. We are deeply convinced that not a single book has been written on this subject. If there has, we haven't been able to find it. Time and time again people asked us: "Why don't you write the book yourselves?" Margriet would then point in my direction, because I am deemed to be the writing element in our relationship. That is why, at the request and insistence of a lot of people, this book was written. We had a title very quickly: "Reading Toes".

By the way, I've been able to put off the actual writing for years – until the moment when I was careless enough to tell a publisher something about toe-reading. He appeared to be very interested. At first I thought he was just being friendly, and that he would never mention it again. I had to adjust that thought, after I had had a look at his toes. My publisher gave me time to elaborate the theory of toe-reading and to find people who wanted their feet to be photographed and interpreted. I was also given time to overcome my 'teething troubles' because the real start remained difficult!

I asked my good friend Jan Schilt of "De Loods" (some years ago this was a centre where all kinds of alternative courses were given) if he could help me. He could and he would. What I needed were people who would "lend" us their feet for publication. The result was that in two days Margriet and I looked at more than forty pairs of feet and analyzed them. Ted Sluymer took the pictures. We told the owners our findings and noted their comments. Everything was tape-recorded, and typed out on an Amstrad laptop computer by my son Ferri, sitting in the sun in the summer holidays. My oldest son Sandor must also be mentioned because he regularly drew my attention to the changing position of his toes while he was wrestling his way through puberty. As he grew more loud-mouthed and learned how to stand up for himself, the shape and position of his toes changed. With his toes especially we have been able to see how much the toes are a "mirror of personality and the soul". Keeping up with his inner development and the development of his toes has convinced me that there is an obvious relationship between behaviour and the inner self of people, and the position of their toes. This stimulated me very much to go as deeply into the matter as possible.

I would very much like to thank all the people who have inspired me, but also those who have contradicted me vigorously. Without them "Reading Toes" would never have been published. You would-n't be reading this either if my dear friend, journalist Ellen Eggels, had not been prepared to act as the big stick, as a critical reader and as a fine filter for my abundance of words and ideas.

Now it only remains for me to ask the reader something: If this book should ever inspire you to practise toe-reading yourself, please be mild in your interpretations. I have noticed regularly that I become so fascinated with crooked, deviant toe positions, that I am inclined to overemphasize the negative aspects. Those that are "out of step" do attract more attention than aspects in harmony. "Strange" toes have a past of suppressed feelings, frustrations and hidden emotions. But the beautiful straight toes do tell their story too. They stand for equilibrium and a positive attitude; natural control and settled emotions and energy. A responsible interpretation points out possibilities and impossibilities, strengths and weaknesses. A good interpretation never gives a value judgement, but holds a mirror up to someone's face. And good mirrors never distort.

IMRE SOMOGYI

Chapter One
The Beginning

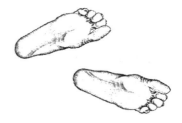

In my life it has often occurred that I had a burning question to which, whatever I did, I could not find an answer. Once I became reconciled to this, the answer often presented itself spontaneously. At one point in my life I read a mystical explanation for this phenomenon: "If you want your wishes or prayers to come true, you will have to let them go. You cannot keep them with you, for nothing will happen." You could compare it with someone at the counter in a post office who does not give the text of his telegram to the counter clerk. If you want to despatch a message you will have to let the text slip go and trust that the Post Office will do its job and deliver the telegram to the correct address. Only when you release a 'message', disengage yourself from it, will it be dealt with in the proper way. In cosmic terms: "Thoughts have to be sent off in the trust and faith that they will be dealt with on a higher level."

I often thought of this during the search for a theory which could be the basis for the relationship of the position of toes to the character of a person. In the libraries I visited I did not find very much, nor did I meet anyone with some beautiful thoughts on the subject. At the very moment that I decided to give up my ambition to read toes after a lot of fruitless research, I heard somebody tell an unusual version of the story of the Creation. That story occupied my mind for quite a while. I was fascinated by it and it offered a sound basis which enabled me to sort out my stray thoughts concerning a theory about the phenomenon of toe-reading. In so far as I could ascertain, the version I was told was derived from the Bible, the Thorah, the Talmud and the Ayurveda. In the following months I analyzed and checked the story in every particular. I discussed it with several people and discovered new aspects which helped me with the foundation of a theory on toe-reading. I will try to summarize the story for you:

"At the root of creation lies an infinitely large neutral force. In the beginning this 'primal force' transmits from its core an energy with a positive (Yang) charge. This positive, outward force is the basis of the entire creation. As creation proceeds, this force condenses. The gas formed thickens to liquid which then crystallizes into dense matter. From this matter in turn come all possible sorts of minerals, vegetables and animals.

In the end the man Adam is the most complex and advanced form of crystallization. There is a duality in creation. Every pole gets its antipole. So besides the positive outward energy (Yang), a negative (Yin) receptive force is called into being. From Adam, the man, a female form is created as an antipole: Eve. Because of this a division in the primal force in which Yin and Yang are united takes place. A division of positive and negative, light and dark, sun and moon, heaven and earth, land and water, male and female. Male energy has always represented outgoing energy, creation. The female stands for the receptive in the cosmos. When the positive and negative forces are equally active, this will automatically lead to harmony, to neutrality, equal to the image of the Creating Primal Force.

The first habitat of man and woman is the Garden of Eden or Paradise. In the centre of Paradise are two trees: the tree of life and the tree of knowledge of good and evil. According to this story, Paradise is the symbol of the human body.

The Garden of Eden lies between the eyebrows. The roots of the two trees sprout in the centre of the Garden of Eden, in the head, in the brain. The stems are made up by the spinal column. The tree of life is the antipole of the tree of knowledge of good and evil, which bears five fruits. In paradise male and female energy are united in harmony, until the moment when the thirst for knowledge gets the upper hand. The woman understood that first. That is why the female energy freed itself from the blissful state of mind in the centre of Paradise first. She is the first one to eat a fruit from the tree of knowl-

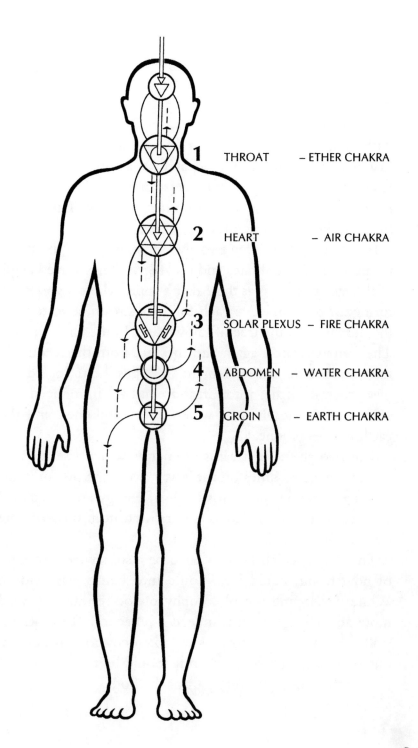

1 THROAT   – ETHER CHAKRA

2 HEART   – AIR CHAKRA

3 SOLAR PLEXUS – FIRE CHAKRA

4 ABDOMEN   – WATER CHAKRA

5 GROIN   – EARTH CHAKRA

edge, which is symbolized by an apple. Then, outside Paradise, she gets acquainted with the element ether. That is where she feels joy for the new but at the same time grief over the separation from Adam and the loss of harmony. In an attempt to restore harmony, Adam is invited to join Eve and taste of the first fruit of knowledge as well. In the ether they find each other again and there they are confronted with their first emotion. Their energy mixes on the spot where the first fruit of knowledge is located, the throat. The joy over their reunion and the sorrow at their departure from Paradise mix. Now that they have left Paradise there is no turning back. There is nothing else for them but to proceed further into Creation.

In the Garden of Eden two rivers rise, which in the Bible are compared with the Euphrates and the Tigris. They leave Paradise by way of the eyes and cross at the Adam's apple where a vortex of energy is formed. Adam and Eve each follow a stream, a vortex, in search of the next fruit of the tree of knowledge. In the chest they meet again. Their energy mixes again and they eat from the second fruit which introduces them to the element air. Thus the male and female energies proceed further into Creation and are introduced to fire in the solar plexus, the element water in the abdomen and the element earth in the tailbone.

The two rivers or streams of energy, which rise in Paradise, cross one another five times on their way along the tree of knowledge. In Eastern literature these crossroads of energy are called chakras. Our western staff of Aesculapius is borrowed from this symbolism of the tree of knowledge."

This story, which I consider to be a somewhat free interpretation of how things could have come into being, has made me think. While developing the philosophy of toe-reading I have discovered more analogies. If man is indeed a reflection of Creation, if it is all really like this - macrocosmos and microcosmos, up and down, in and out, as above, so below - then it should be possible to find a reflection of the whole in every part of the body.

Chapter Two
Reading The Body

Time and time again we come across the proposition that in every part of the body we can find a reflection of the whole.

In ear acupuncture it is assumed that the auricle is a reflection of a fetus, thus providing a chart with the corresponding areas.

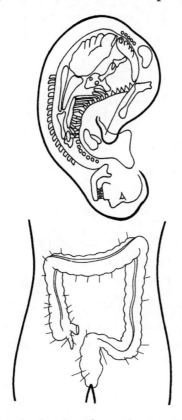

In intestinal therapy the body of a snake is projected onto the large intestine and the reflex points can be found in the neck.

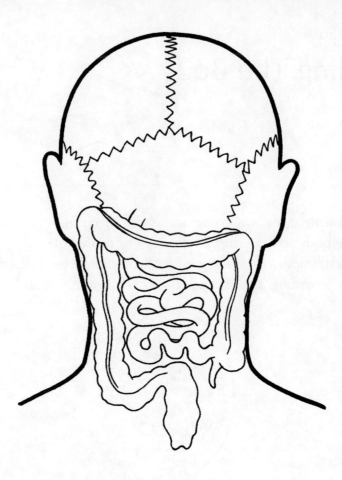

When the neck is massaged for a long period, quite a lot of activity starts up in the intestine. Thus we can conclude that unsuspected reflex points are located in the neck. Therapists have discovered that pain in the neck is, more often than not, accompanied by a bothersome accumulation of flatus and bad bowels. A 'map' of the intestines can be superimposed on the neck, showing various reflex points.

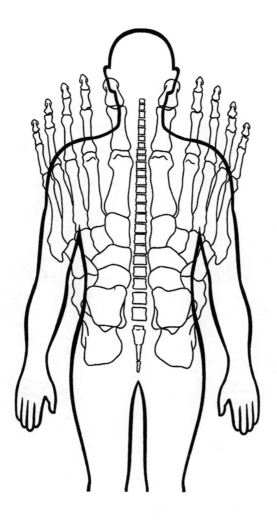

A projection of the bone structure of the foot, superimposed on the human body. Podologists assume that defects in the body can be influenced by a minimal manipulation of the skeleton of the foot. An adjustment by means of a small inner sole can bring about an improvement in posture, health and state of mind.

In foot reflexology reflections of the body's two halves can be found in each foot.

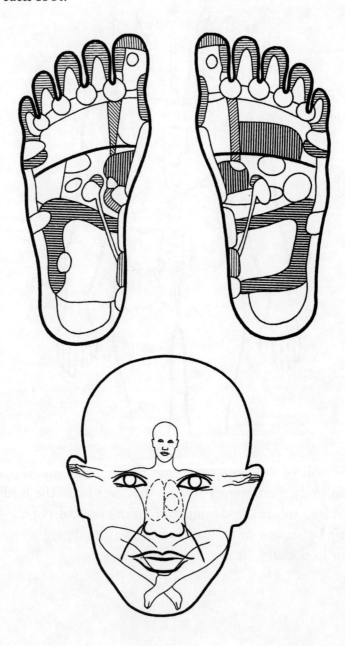

Facial diagnostics by way of a reflection of the whole body in the face.

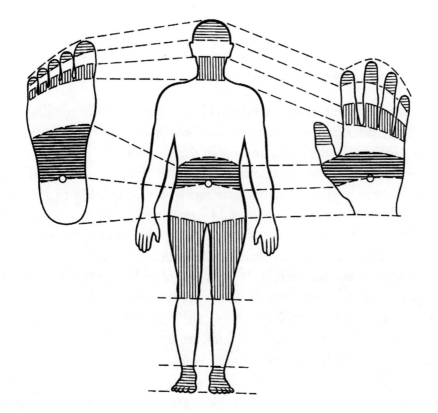

Dr. Randolph Stone, father of the polarity therapy, divides the body into zones. The body (macro) is reflected in hands and feet (micro).

So-called 'body-readers' in the United States state that physical and mental stress leads to a certain posture. By analyzing this posture they can make a diagnosis.

After having studied all these theories I gradually accepted the idea that 'everything' is a reflection of 'everything'. Thus toes must reflect the whole body. The shape and position of the toes could symbolize (deviant) energy patterns and mirror stress in body and mind.

Chapter Three
Chakras or Centres of Energy

Until now I have not told you anything concrete about reading toes. However, do not fear! A small dose of theory and clarification is essential for a good understanding of the subject.

It would be something else if I were reading your toes myself. The very moment you uncovered your feet I would be able to see what kind of toes appeared and it would be possible for me to give you my first analysis. If you master toe-reading, it is possible to reveal the essence of someone's inner life in a few sentences. The first impression is almost always correct. It does not matter whether I have seen the person in question before or not. It is even possible to read toes from a photograph, although that has limitations. You cannot see how the toes move nor can you look under them.

Most people whose toes are read show the same reaction: "How can you know so much about me despite the fact that you don't know me at all?" It is not very different from astrologists or palm readers. A couple of pointed remarks and people get curious and you have undivided attention. Toe-reading is just like writing an interesting article: first an arresting headline, and then an eye-catching opening sentence. Only then do you go into further detail.

The greatest problem I encounter time and time again while editing this book is that I can't surprise you with a few striking observations and remarks about your inner life. This would catch your undivided attention and tempt you to finish this book in one go. I can't see your feet, I can't draw you in with the remark that you are immune to stress. That you stick up for yourself when you don't like something. Or that you bottle everything up and let yourself be walked all over the whole time. I would have told you the latter if I had seen that your big toes came to a point. My closest friend (not to be confused with my wife Margriet) has toes like that. She has beautiful toes which, in general, point straight forward, but her big toes don't look too good. She is a worrier, bottling everything up. I have never seen her cry. She 'swallows' everything immediately.

Are you with me on this? This friend of mine has had problems with her throat for years because she doesn't deal properly with emotions that settle in the throat. She has been under the doctor for quite a while, but that doesn't work. She has to adopt a different attitude to life. I can't help her with that. I simply establish the fact.

Why do we need a long introduction again? I hope that by mentioning examples and telling you how toe-reading works for me, the matter will come alive for you.

It's time for some basic theory. First we deal with the chakras. CHAKRAS OR CENTRES OF ENERGY Chakra means 'wheel' in Sanskrit and may be used to refer to the five physical centres of energy in the body. These chakras stand for the five fruits on the tree of knowledge, in the Garden of Eden. They are the points where the male Yang energy and the female Yin energy meet in a whirl, spinning like a wheel on its axle. If you have ever studied Eastern medicine, you will be familiar with the phenomenon. If not I will summarize it for you.

We won't bother with the mental chakra, which is situated in the head between the eyebrows, because it is not reflected in the feet. Paradise is perfection, equilibrium, absolute harmony. This energy is not earthly and is not found in matter, in creation, in man. The five physical chakras are the centres where emotions originate from.

The chakra that is connected with the ether, the most rarefied form of energy, is situated in the larynx, or the throat. This is where we come across joy and sorrow. Both are inextricably bound up with life and can alternate rapidly sometimes. Crying one minute and laughing the next. From having a lump in one's throat from grief to shouting with joy. Joy and sorrow are not appreciated equally in our western society. Generally, people don't have too much of a problem

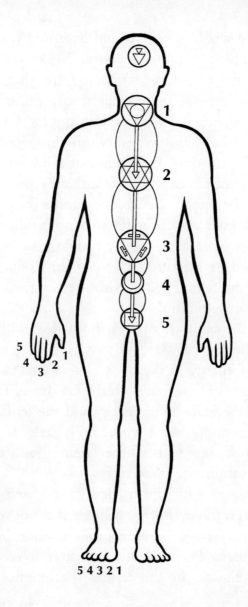

ELEMENT	RIGHT MALE	LEFT FEMALE
1 ETHER	JOY	SORROW
2 AIR	DESIRE	EMOTIONS
3 FIRE	AGGRESSION	CREATIVITY
4 WATER	ATTACHMENT	LOVE
5 EARTH	FEAR	TRUST

with joy. Sorrow, on the other hand, is something else. Yet sorrow, like all other emotions, should be expressed freely.

Crying loudly during mourning ceremonies, which is quite common in various cultures, is regarded as excessive in our civilized western culture. Yet this crying has a very positive function: sorrow has to get out before there is room for joy. Anyone who bottles up and swallows the sorrow will undoubtedly end up with problems, just like my friend. Phrases like 'having a lump in one's throat' obviously have a deeper meaning. See how people at funerals are manfully trying to swallow their tears with a lump in their throats. When an emotion is kept for a long time, the emotion thickens, crystallizes as it were, and settles on the spot where the emotion originated from. This process appears to occur in various reflex points, like in the foot. The reflex becomes painful. We have discovered that, during the process of crystallization, the positions of the toes change as well. What happens in the area of the throat will be reflected in the big toe. After dealing with either sorrow or joy there will always be a void. Everybody knows the empty feeling after a fit of weeping or after an animated party when you're alone again. The emptiness arising in the ether will automatically be filled with new energies from the chakra of the heart.

As we descend we find the chakra of the heart in the chest. This chakra is connected with the element air. This is where wish or desire (right) and the antipole emotions (left) reside. When someone hurts your feelings you feel "stabbed in the heart". The expression "having your heart's desire" also originates from what happens in the chakra of the heart, or the chakra of air. Anyone who handles the energy in the chakra of the heart not quite naturally can, in the long run, feel like gasping for air. When there are long-term blockages in the chakra of the heart, sometimes complaints of the heart and lungs occur. The air chakra is reflected in both second toes.

Below the centre of the heart lies the Solar Plexus. This centre of fire is a strong chakra where creative energy originates from. Here aggression and creativity vibrate. Wishes, desires and expressions of creativity need fire energy or aggression in order to be realized. We find creativity on the left side and aggression on the right, on the side of the gall-bladder and the liver. It is because of this that we have expressions like "venting one's spleen". If someone "vents his spleen", he expresses what bothers him. We don't have an expression for creativity as far as I know, regrettably.

But nevertheless the condition of your fire energy can be read from the position of your middle toes.

Next stop is the water chakra, in the lower abdomen. This represents love and at the same time attachment. Anyone who loves too passionately can cling to someone too violently sometimes. Anyone who loves sincerely will be able to let the object of his love go. It is from this kind of love that well-balanced mothers give their children enough freedom to develop themselves. Beautifully straight fourth toes indicate that this person manages to balance the Yin and the Yang in the water chakra. Mothers who cannot detach themselves from their growing children literally have crooked toes when the apples of their eyes, the objects of their care, eventually leave the nest. They are the ones who often go to the doctor with complaints in the lower abdomen. When love changes into possessiveness, the most extreme form of attachment turns into jealousy.

Now only the earth chakra in the groin remains. We have now reached a point where subtle energy has crystallized into a more dense shape. Optimism, trust in the future and fear are found here. But so is the most earthly expression of love – sex. Maybe it seems strange to you that sex and trust are reflected together in one toe. But you have to realize that at the very moment when someone reaches the sexual climax, there is a second or so of total helplessness. There is no room for thought there. Just before, and while reaching, the sexual climax, people are defenceless, and therefore need to trust. Without trust sexuality can't be worked out. That is why they belong to each other.

Lack of trust is a form of insecurity which in the worst case can lead to anxiety. To indicate where the phenomenon fear is situated, we have the expressions: "To run off with your tail between your legs"…and "to shit yourself with fear". Insecurity and fear of failure can also be camouflaged with a pompous attitude and a lot of blah blah. As I said in the introduction, when I see a macho man with a puffed-up chest parading on the beach, I bet with 99% certainty that he is afraid and insecure about his own personality and the game between the sheets. His scrunched-up, hidden little toes do show this. From the position of these toes you can read how someone deals not only with fear and sexuality, but optimism and trust as well.

All male, rational emotions are on the right side of the body and in the right foot. The female, intuitive emotions are on the left. In the chakras the two polarities or streams of life cross. When Yin and Yang are in balance there is health and harmony.

The moment that the energy flows are blocked, the energy accumulates, condenses, crystallizes and results in pain in the body and in the toes. The longer the emotions are held onto, the harder the spot becomes, and the more sharply the pain will manifest itself. At the same time the toes assume more crooked and distorted positions. The good toe-reader can hold up a mirror to someone's face. Whether the person in question modifies his behaviour after that is his decision entirely.

CHAKRAS OR CENTRES OF ENERGY

Chapter Four

Position of the Toes: Mirror of the Inner Self

When I state that stable persons have beautiful, evenly-shaped toes and that somewhat less stable people are really 'toe-tied', people always say that I am talking nonsense. My critics are of the opinion that incorrectly-positioned toes are caused by wearing the wrong shoes, and that inner life has nothing to do with it. I am never taken aback by remarks like that. I even think that there is a very close connection between character, behaviour and attitude to life and the choice of certain footwear. I always point out therefore that in ancient times Chinese men decided that women with little feet were the acme of beauty. In order to meet that ideal of beauty the feet of little girls were swathed to stunt their growth. For generations Chinese women submitted themselves to ideals devised by man. And the men knew exactly what they were doing!

People who cannot spread their feet in a normal fashion while they are walking literally lack a firm foundation. Simply moving demands great effort because they must struggle constantly to maintain balance. This results in an unsteady gait. When someone has to concentrate on keeping her balance, there will automatically be less attention for other matters. Walking in awkward shoes costs so much energy that little is left for other activities. After a day of shopping in high heels women tend to say: "All I want now is a nice foot-bath because my feet are killing me!" That is the price one pays for 'beauty'. We do not have the expression "No pain, no gain" for nothing. Anyone who has had pain or been troubled by something for quite some time will know that the inner self and one's way of thinking are to a large extent influenced by such matters.

By the way, in our Western culture we also know something about manipulation of the body. On Crete drawings have been found from the time of King Minos, in which women are depicted with abnormally slender waists. The women probably achieved such slender waists by lacing themselves up with leather. When in the eighteenth and nineteenth centuries the ladies laced themselves up in literally breathtaking corsets, there was nothing new under the sun. It seems that around the turn of the century men joined in with the ladies. By using a corset they changed their entire torso so that they would get a puffed-up, masculine chest.

Even today we find examples of manipulation in fashion. Shoe designers especially are in a position that enables them to manipulate people vigorously. They can give people a firm basis or deprive them of one. There was a time when they let women walk on four-inch heels, with a base of less than 0.15 square inch. Women who wear shoes like that literally walk on their toes to keep up with fashion. People walking on their toes do their utmost to subordinate themselves to a situation or someone else. In prostitution this kind of footwear is still used. It is often associated with subordination and servitude, although in many cases not on purpose.

In the book "Modern Foot Care" from M & P Weert Publishers I read the following sentence: "The battle between fashion and health often ends with a victory for fashion and therefore a defeat for the feet." However, there are times when people do choose a firm foundation for their feet. That is when loafers come back into fashion. In the seventies you had crepe-soled shoes, plump and wide with ample space for the toes. That image matched developments in society. People rebelled against power and establishment. People wanted nothing to do with authority, let alone fashion. They wanted to make decisions of their own and declare themselves independent. Punks wore steelcapped shoes. They seemed to symbolize the fact that he who wore them could not be hurt even if society stepped right on his toes.

Towards the end of the eighties people appeared to care hardly at all about fashion. The individual emerged strongly. People felt less need to conform to an idealized image. Once again the loafer came into fashion. This is a shoe which enables the foot to make full contact with the earth. In my opinion, what it all comes down to is that people who allow their feet to be deformed and their toes to be manipulated until they are crooked are the kind who allow other people to impose on them rules and standards which run counter to their own personalities. Crooked toes show how in the ends (of the toes) one's own energy is flushed down the drain and flows away into the earth. This indicates an inward attitude of resignation and of giving up resistance against anything that is considered to be stronger. When certain toes are put under pressure they will eventually cause an inward reaction. On the other hand I found that when someone changes inwardly, the toes change accordingly, even at an advanced age.

Chapter Five

The Development of the Foot

Between the eighteenth and twenty-first years of one's life the bone structure of the feet completes its development. So the formation of the feet runs parallel to the process of physical maturing. When man has fully grown, the foot has as well. That does not mean that the foot, and especially the toes, cannot change along with the inner self.

Infant feet show very well that the front of the foot is broad and the heel narrow, so that toes need a lot of space. Wearing too tight socks, too tight shoes or a pair of rompers that is too tight can affect the growth of feet adversely. Free feet develop best. No matter how trendy, the practice of making children wear a pair of fashionable jogging shoes in the play pen is a fundamental limitation on the energy of children. The growth of children's feet should never be hindered. Parents should keep in mind that children's feet are still so soft that they rarely hurt when they are squeezed into too tight shoes. You won't hear a child complain very soon. Yet there are children who are already in such close touch with their bodies at a young age that they won't be palmed off with too tight footwear under any circumstances. I will give you the example of two brothers, a ten-year-old and a five-year-old. It is the dead of winter, and the snow lies thick everywhere. Both of them play outside for a while in their everyday leather shoes. At one point their mother calls them inside for a cup of tea. When they want to go outside again, the leather shoes turn out to be soaked. Mother insists that her sons put on gumboots. The oldest brother complains that they are too small, because they are from last year. Still he puts them on and goes outside. The youngest of the two tries his on, considers them too tight and wants to put on his wet shoes. His mother won't allow him, and he decides to stay inside. When his mother doesn't pay attention, he sneaks out, and plays on in his socks…Neither wet shoes, nor too tight boots, nor his mother's "Don't!" can stop him. His brother plays in his too tight boots all afternoon.

I am often touched by the image of toes. Sometimes I fall silent when I see so much love, or so much aggression, sorrow or fear. I have rarely been moved by feet. One time I was, and I burst into tears. That happened when a colleague of mine showed me a picture of her newborn son's little feet. Never before or since have I seen a pair of feet this balanced. Completely symmetric. Toes as straight as arrows that radiated flexibility. Never broadening or narrowing and perfect nails with almost angular tips. I was flabbergasted. This baby was born with an unprecedented built-in equilibrium. This child, I predicted, will do exactly what it wants from the day of its birth. He won't allow anyone or anything to stand in his way. The flexibility of his little feet, which was confirmed by his mother, indicates a great talent to bend people and things to his will. I was doubly touched when I realized what it means to parents to have a child like this one. Being confronted right from day one with a person who stands his ground. Having to ask yourself constantly whether what you impose or refuse is reasonable during the process of bringing him up.

For, when the child decides it is best for him to turn in at eleven o'clock, you, as a parent, will have to bring a gallon of chloroform and a sledgehammer to send him to Morpheus' world at an earlier time. He will keep on whining until eleven o'clock and only then will he give in and go to sleep. General rules don't apply for such a kid. The only thing that counts for him is his own inner rhythm and the development of abilities.

Now, six years later, Christiaan's mother tells me regularly how correct that first observation was. Christiaan is an extremely well-balanced little fellow, who can hardly be influenced, if at all. He started talking when he was two years old, apparently quite deliberately because he didn't first try a few babbled words, like most toddlers, to practise on. No, he immediately used well-turned and grammatically correct sentences. He will get on. His parents can be proud of him in advance. A lot of adaptability is demanded of them, however, for their own Christiaan has easily got the better of them ever since he was born. Observing something like that in a single glance moves me.

On the other hand, the deforming of feet isn't always influenced by external factors. Sometimes a child is born with deviant feet and toes. I know an extremely optimistic man who was born with two little toes on his left foot. He is the kind of man who tells you today that he goes away on vacation tomorrow, but he doesn't have any money and not the slightest idea where he's going. When you call him the next day, he appears not to be home. A month later he pops up again and tells the most unbelievable stories: "…worked on a boat and invited by a millionaire", etc. When you check up on those stories they prove to be true. This man has double helpings of both optimism and faith in the future.

Chapter Six

Which Toe Represents What?

In toe-reading we assume that each toe reflects a certain emotion or energy. The shape and position of the toes show how the owner deals with his energies, or how his chakras are doing.

Just a little more theory and then it's off with your shoes and socks and we will get to work, for then the fun part begins. Your own feet show what you're made of.

The big toes represent the element ether. The next toes stand for air, fire, water and earth. Air, fire, water and earth are found in creation. Creation itself is the ether.

We can chart these elements with their respective emotions (chapter 3) with the following diagram:

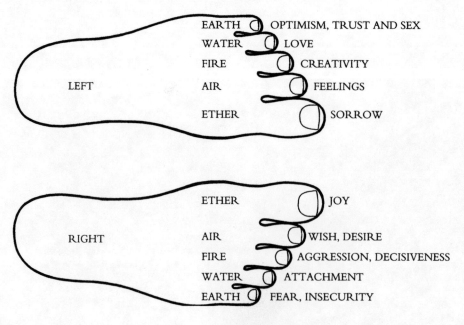

LEFT		
EARTH		OPTIMISM, TRUST AND SEX
WATER		LOVE
FIRE		CREATIVITY
AIR		FEELINGS
ETHER		SORROW

RIGHT		
ETHER		JOY
AIR		WISH, DESIRE
FIRE		AGGRESSION, DECISIVENESS
WATER		ATTACHMENT
EARTH		FEAR, INSECURITY

The elements air, fire, water and earth can only manifest themselves when they are brought into the ether.

Example: You don't know if someone is angry unless he expresses his anger. The aggression has to be brought into the ether. There are two ways of doing that. The direct way is to move the aggression straight to the throat and to yell (Yang: rationally) or to cry (Yin: instinctively) with anger.

The indirect way is to cope with it. The aggression moves from the solar plexus (the centre of fire) to the chakras of the belly and the tail-bone and will be brought into the ether by way of the natural cycle of energy.

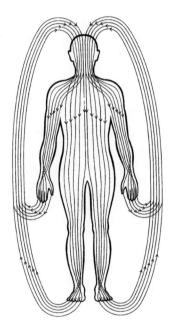

WHICH TOE REPRESENTS WHAT?

The indirect way of expressing feelings can be sedate because the emotion has been digested partly on the way, so to speak. However, when there are some old sores left, when something still sticks in the throat, this can be sucked out. This will trigger a second, delayed airing, which can prove to be way out of proportion.

We may say, without depreciating the other toes, that the big toes are very important. The positions of these toes, their shape and the proportion to the other toes can tell us a lot about their owner.

Chapter Seven

The Big Ether-Toes

When the make-up of a foot is similar to that of the one depicted in diagram A, ether and the other elements are in absolute harmony. All energies can be brought into the ether in a stable way. The big toe is the sum of the other toes. You can put a ruler to toes like that.

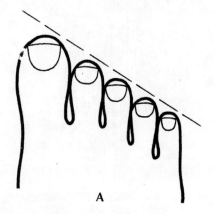

A

When you are confronted with a big toe like the one in diagram B, it belongs to someone with a relatively small ether. The big toe is short in proportion to the other toes. The ether is too confined. Because the proportions are out of balance, chaos arises quickly. When there is too much information from the other toes, the other centres of energy, flowing towards the ether, there will be a 'traffic jam'. When the owner of these toes wants to express his feelings and all that is happening in his mind, you will end up in a terrible mess. The energies will crowd to be the first one in the ether. Here you are dealing with someone who rambles from one subject to another. Someone like that can swamp you with twenty ideas at a time, and is probably busy carrying out at least half of them.

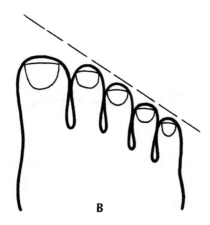

B

An extremely large big toe (diagram C) shows that the ether is too big. The energies that end up in there literally swim in it. They don't pass through in a structured way. Someone with toes like that talks constantly. He does not care what about as long as he can keep on talking. These verbal explosions are hardly ever based on a level-headed sense of reality. To put it plainly: "he's full of hot air".

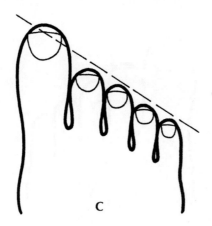

C

35

A big toe with a rectangular shape as shown in diagram D belongs to someone who says things 'in plain terms'.

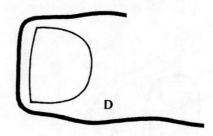

Diagram E represents someone who softens the edges of his remarks when they're brought into the ether. This results in gentle, sensitive and tactful behaviour.

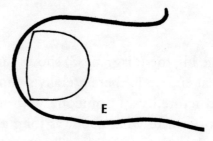

The most natural arrangement would be when the toes are in immediate contact with each other as shown in diagram F. The energy flows smoothly from one chakra to the next.

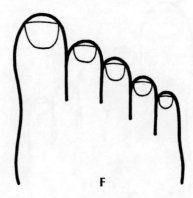

Diagram G shows a clear diversion. The big toe stands apart. A person with a big toe standing apart like that needs time before he can express himself. The bigger the gap between the big toe and the other toes, the longer it takes before the external world shares in thoughts and feelings. The dots symbolize the diversion the energy is forced to make before it will come into the ether.

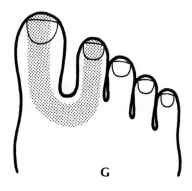

G

THE BIG
ETHER-TOES

37

Chapter Eight

A Basic Guide to Toe-Reading

What kind of toes can we come across and what do they tell us?

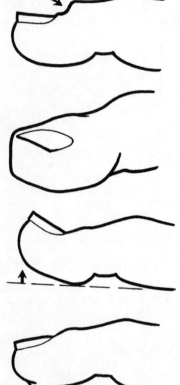

1. Flattened tip: Expressing feelings or intellectual considerations in a modest but emphatic manner.

2. Block-shaped: The energy reflected in a block-shaped toe will eventually be put to use in a blunt way. Undeniably unpliable and with the heels dug in, a dominating presence. The message reads: no bargaining possible. Bend or break.

3. Dream toe: The tip of a dream toe is not in contact with the ground. This pattern indicates daydreaming, imagination, and a potential for shirking reality.

4. Drop shape: A toe with a drop under it hides a feature from the view of the observer. There is a lot of hidden energy.

5. Bunion: Bunions indicate that the expression of an emotion will be partly obscured from view. If someone does something he or she, for some reason, does not think appropriate you will often find a bunion on the toe related to expressing that emotion.

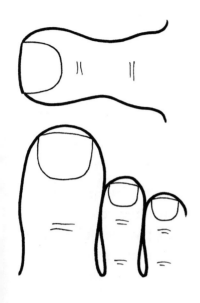

6. Bottleneck: A toe with a bottleneck shape looks as though someone has squeezed it, revealing that the energy is stalled temporarily and behaving like a car in a traffic jam. There is no possibility of increasing speed.

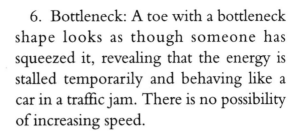

7. Large big toes: People with large big toes are very articulate speakers. They talk much and long.

8. Twisted: A twisted toe indicates that there is a change of direction "en route". When a toe is tilted there is a "different" attitude than usual from the beginning. In a twisted toe at first (at the root) there is a recognizable reaction, but later on the direction changes, and the outside world doesn't recognize the original energy any more. The originally offered energy is denied, and presented as if from another source.

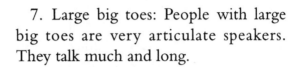

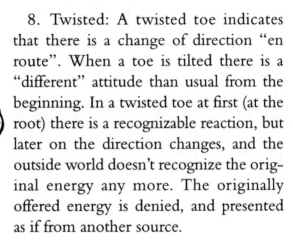

9. Tilted: Here something different is presented, from what the owner actually thinks and feels. A tilt causes different behaviour, a different handling of the energy from the way it was originally intended.

10. Crooked: Toes so crooked that they adjust themselves to the line (big toe – little toe) indicate a capacity for manipulation.

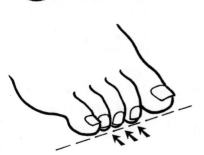

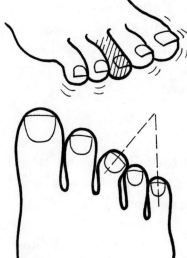

11. Tense toe: A toe that feels tense indicates that there is a big change taking place: an effort to change a pattern. Very often a toe like that has a different colour from the other toes because of increased activity and energy.

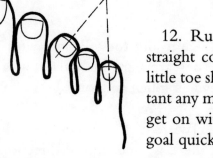

12. Rush-toe: A toe deviating from its straight course and inclined towards the little toe shows that the past is not important any more, and that there is a hurry to get on with the future. Eager to reach a goal quickly.

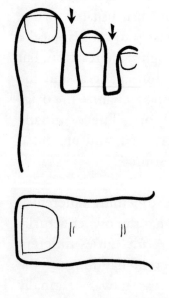

13. Gap: A gap is wider than a wedge and shows that two energies hardly communicate with each other, if at all.

14. Toe with angular tip: This indicates a way of expressing energy intransigently. Doesn't feel like being tactful. Too bad if this bothers anybody. That's the way I am, and I don't want to change it.

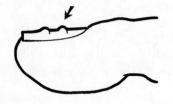

15. Horizontal ripple-marks on the toenails: Wave-like motion in the emotional field. The energy connected with the toe whose nail has ripple-marks causes emotional instability.

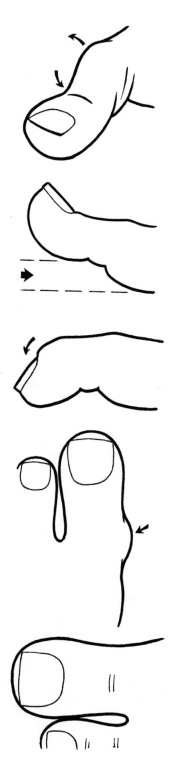

16. Withdrawn toes (or the ability to withdraw them): The extent to which a person can manipulate (or postpone statements or announcements) can be gathered from the ability (or lack of it) to withdraw the toes as shown in the picture.

17. Upturned toe: An upturned toe points into the air. The toe is not earthed. This causes groundless arguments, fantasies and daydreaming. This position of a toe doesn't cause any problems, and is often experienced as a welcome way of escaping reality.

18. Clawing toe: This happens when the outside world has enforced restraint or when someone from the outside world with a lot of dominant power doesn't accept certain ways in which the owner expresses himself.

19. Lump at the root of the big toe (side of the foot): This indicates self-effacement, helpfulness. When this is strongly present, with a deviant position of the toe (this is called Hallux Valgus), self-effacement is at the cost of the owner. It shows that personal interests are made subordinate to those of others.

20. Left ether-toe: Through the left ether-toe all female, emotional matters are expressed. The emotion connected with the left ether-toe is sorrow.

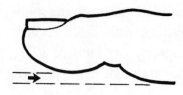

21. Not earthed: The tip of a toe that is not earthed does not make contact with the ground. The energy belonging to the toe is not expressed on rational grounds (someone with an activity-toe that is not earthed cannot explain why he gets angry). To the outside world, these outbursts seem incomprehensible. If, on top of that, the toe can be moved in such a way that the tip points entirely into the air, this indicates the ability to daydream and to fantasize problems away.

22. Depressed rounded toes: A rounded toe depressed under another toe indicates modesty. At the same time it means stimulation of, even putting pressure on, the energy connected with the toe. This provides a good grounding which eliminates the inclination to daydream and fantasize.

23. Depressed spatula-shaped toes: A spatula-shaped toe depressed under another toe tells us: "It's none of your damn business. I go my way and put pressure on myself." This results from putting the energy connected with the toe to the ground, earthing it. This stifles the urge to wander off, and stimulates the strength to act.

24. Depressed pointy toes: Pointy toes, depressed under other toes, hide. It looks as though the energy isn't there, but sometimes the energy comes out sharply, only to be denied for the larger part afterwards.

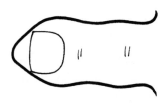

25. Pointy: A wedge-shaped toe represents a way of expressing the energy connected with the toe sharply and penetratively. No stable, balanced expression but an unexpectedly harsh one, like a bolt from the blue. Tense.

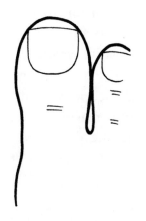

26. Right ether-toe: Through the right ether-toe all male, rational matters are expressed. The emotion connected with the right ether-toe is joy.

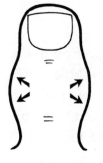

27. Reservoir: The shape of a reservoir indicates bottled-up energy.

28. Rounded shape: A toe with a round tip indicates that the edges of expressions are softened before they are brought into the ether. A round shape can be interpreted as tactical by nature, docile or fearful of voicing one's own opinion.

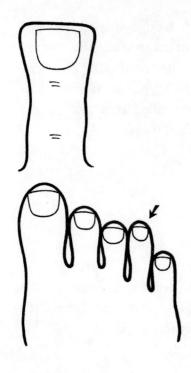

29. Spatula shape: Spatula shapes indicate that eventually (the spatula always comes at the tip of a toe) a lot of energy will be expressed. This often happens in an unexpectedly powerful way.

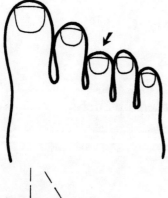

30. Toe too big in proportion to the overall picture: Lots of energy, lots of activity. People with positive attitudes take advantage of this increased energy and stimulate their other energies with it. Negative-minded people reason away this energy or even become depressed, because everything they feel bubbling up doesn't lead to anything.

31. Toe too small in proportion to the overall picture: Little energy, little activity. Positive-minded people will make an extra effort to "straighten out". People with a negative attitude are inclined to ignore the energy.

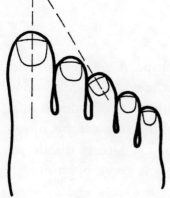

32. Retro-toe (looking back): A toe deviating from its straight "course" and inclined towards the big toe indicates looking back and drawing parallels with the past.

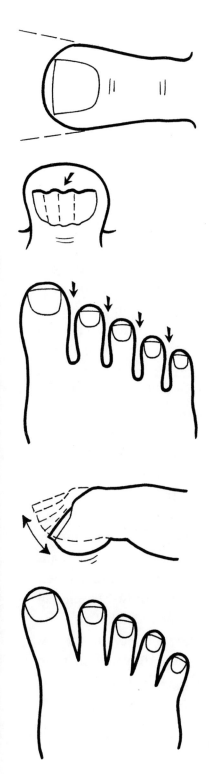

33. Broadening: A toe that becomes broader indicates a gradually more energetic approach and growing confidence as a process progresses.

34. Vertical ripple-marks on the toenails: Vertical ripple-marks indicate metabolic disorders. When they appear on only one toenail, there often is a relationship between the toe on which they appear, and the part of the body that is connected with it.

35. Small spaces between the toes: When a situation requires an immediate reaction, it can often be given. But the spaces, which are there by nature, reveal constant reconsideration and reflection. They also represent inner uncertainty.

36. Toe at work: This often occurs when a seemingly static clawing toe turns out to be flexible after all. When this is the case, there is always an internal change going on. This also applies to toes that look stiff, but turn out to be flexible after all. A toe at work can be distinguished by its redder colour.

37. Wedge: This is a v-shaped space between the toes, indicating that processes elapse very slowly, and direct, impulsive expressions are out of the question. Stands for thinking, acting or feeling at one remove.

Chapter Nine
Relationship Between Health and the Position of the Toes

This chapter is about the connection that can be made between the position of the toes and blockages of energy.

Before I go on, I think it's best to point the following out to you. Many physical defects of the feet can occur, which make it impossible to read toes reliably. Complications after fractions, exostosis (morbid growth of the bone), rheumatism, etc. etc., have such a big influence that a reliable interpretation of the toes is impossible. I therefore advise you to drop your "hobby" in such cases. When you are reading toes, stick to the "average" feet; you will have your hands more than full with them. When in doubt, stop!

My point of departure is the idea that emotions can cause stress in the body. An example. I am shown the feet of a woman about 45 years old. The toes of the right foot show a balanced picture. On the left foot three toes "step out of line". They are the emotion-toe, the love-toe and the trust-toe. The emotion-toe is perfectly straight until the last phalanx, but then it is bent, at an angle of almost ninety degrees, towards the earth. Her feelings are flushed down the drain completely. The love toe is swollen and red (active), it hurts when touched, and it looks back. The little toe hides almost completely under the love-toe, and its nail is much too small and calcified. The emotional image is clear. Feelings are flushed down the drain, there is too much active love bottled up. This woman often thinks of the time when she was able to express this love. She digs in the past. Her trust is so deeply hidden that she doesn't know how it feels to be optimistic any more, or to express her love (in the sexual field as well). When she has physical complaints, they will occur in the left part of

46

her body. The feelings in the chakra of the heart are flushed down the drain. The culprit is the blocked active love energy. The hidden optimism and the calcified little nail indicate that the energy in the groin is idle. We can assume that the owner of these toes has complaints on the left side of her abdomen, especially as the love-toe is painful and corresponds with the area on the left side of the abdomen. When I inform this woman of the above, she tells me this: she is the mother of a child who, for no apparent reason, constantly rejects all offered affection and care. Worse still, every display of attention is countered with aggression. As a matter of fact, it has been this way since he was born. The feelings of this mother are repeatedly very badly hurt. She can't express her love for her son. She does indeed have continual complaints on the left side of her abdomen. The gynaecologist has diagnosed a cyst on her left ovary, and the cervix has to be watched closely.

When toes deviate from the normal position, this inevitably means something. Accumulations of energy, swelling, redness, drop shapes and calluses, can be seen as reflexes of the corresponding areas of the body. When there is an accumulation of energy, this means that somewhere else there is too little energy. The circulation, the flow, is not balanced. Accumulation or a shortage of energy can, in the long run, when the blockage is not removed, cause physical complaints. Someone who is aware of trouble with the energy balance of the body has the choice whether or not to do anything with the information offered.

It is NOT true, of course, that you can say that someone has an ulcer or a heart condition because of a crooked toe. You have to be very careful when you are making the connection between the position of the toes and physical complaints. Before you know it you are on the slippery slope of quackery. Yet, after a careful study of the toes, you can say where the probable source of someone's physical problems is located.

The thing you ABSOLUTELY can't say anything about is the nature of the ailment. INDICATE LOCATION YES, DIAGNOSIS NO!

By practising toe-reading, in time you will be able to indicate the physical weak spots in a body. YOU MAY NOT AND CANNOT GO ANY FURTHER THAN THAT. Diagnoses have to be made by the medical profession and not by toe-readers. You will often be tempted to say more than you can account for. People whose toes are being read will often ask for very drastic, far-reaching information. With all my heart I hope you will handle the information offered in this book sincerely. When you can read toes well, far too often the aura of being special, maybe even "clairvoyant", will surround you. Do not accept such characterizations. Interpreting the position of the toes is not special, and not mystical at all. Unless someone puts on a show. And nobody needs shows like that, quite the contrary!

READING

TOES

Chapter Ten

Putting Toe-Reading into Practice

In this chapter you will find 17 toe-reading cases. Each one begins with pictures of pairs of feet and lists of the most striking features, followed by our analysis. In toe-reading we start with the right foot, which, by the way, is the left one on the page. This right/left problem can be difficult at first. For your convenience we have made a fold-out front cover. On the inside is a picture with all the toes and their respective elements and emotions.

Toe-reading starts with the big toe on the right foot. Then the adjoining toe and so on. The left foot is also read from the big (ether) toe. The other toes are dealt with from left to right. In chapter 7 I have shown you how important the big toes are for a good interpretation. That is why in the cases I speak of ether toes and not of joy and sorrow toes. The element ether is indispensable in expressing emotions. It is because of this that the emphasis lies with this ether aspect and the emotions joy and sorrow are of secondary importance. On the fourth page of each case you will find the silhouette of a human being. Onto this silhouette a summary of the interpretation of the feet is projected. You will observe that summing up the features can seem cold and even harsh. Without sentences and words to dress it all up a person's inner life can be terribly exposed. Yet I've done this to show you how deep toe-reading can go. Another word of advice: never read other people's toes unless you are prepared to take off your shoes and socks yourself. And finally: never start reading toes that belong to someone else before you have studied and interpreted your own toes thoroughly. Such self-study is essential to be able to read other people's toes in a responsible manner.

For your information: on pages 118 and 119 I have recorded briefly the reactions of the seventeen individuals whose toes were discussed. Their names have been changed.

Barbara – Female – 36 Years

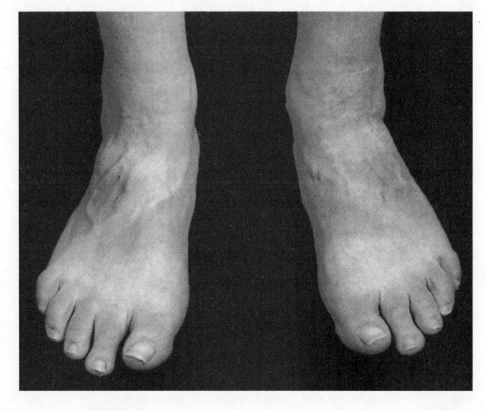

RIGHT	**LEFT**
Big, rounded ether-toe backward-looking	Broad ether-toe with a narrow tip not earthed
Flexible wish-toe bottleneck asymmetric tip spatula shape	Tilted emotion toe with bottleneck asymmetric tip spatula-shaped
Big, stocky, flexible activity-toe	Flexible creativity-toe with drop
Big, flexible and slightly clawing attachment-toe	Static, clawing love-toe
Withdrawn, clawing fear-toe coming to a point	Pointy trust-toe not earthed at the root

Barbara's emotional life is not without bumps. This is shown in the ripple-marks on the nails of her big toes. This instability varies in intensity. There are both small and very large ripple-marks. She herself constantly thinks that she is capable of much more than she actually manages.

The right ether-toe is broad and this indicates a great verbal ability. It only breaks down a bit en route. The tip of the toe comes to a rounded point. There is a turn towards the wish-toe as well. This image shows that Barbara says far less than she actually could and that she often doubts the things she says. You can tell from the gap between the right ether-toe and the wish-toe that there is no primary spontaneous expression. There is no immediate reaction to events. This intensifies the image of doubting even more. Not always rightly so, because in the end Barbara knows exactly what she wants. If, however, you want to know what's on her mind, you'll have to ask today and get your answer tomorrow. The fact that she knows what she wants can be derived from the wish-toe. It starts off with a very broad root. At the outset she wants a great deal, but she has learned that life is full of compromises. The bottleneck is a reflection of easing up a little. However, it is not in her nature to accept 'no' too often. The toe broadens and shows the shape of a spatula at the tip. What Barbara wants, she must have, whatever the impediments. The light asymmetry at the tip of the toe is inclined towards the activity-toe, although there is no constant contact. The wish-toe is tilted slightly towards the activity-toe, although the nail of this toe clearly wants contact with the ether. Rush and agitation appear to enforce quick action. The toe can be manipulated though. We are all familiar with the idea of putting things off to strike better at a later time. The activity-toe is big and stocky. That is the way Barbara works; like a diesel engine. We are dealing with a 'workhorse'. This toe can be manipulated too. Action can be put off. Externally enforced delay of action can make her angry.

When she can be active later on her fit of temper passes and she does not complain about it later. The attachment-toe is very big. Disposing of old things is difficult but not impossible because the attachment-toe can be manipulated well. Despite the fact that it is bent toward earth, there is movement in attachment. There seems to be a process of detachment. You can say, metaphorically, that the junk room used to be stuffed, but can be cleaned out now and then. The fear-toe tries to lead such a withdrawn life that one would almost say that Barbara is afraid of fear. The moment there is turmoil, Barbara tries to withdraw the energy with force. She doesn't always succeed in doing that. The result is fierce, dominating fear and

♀

BARBARA

36 YEARS

51

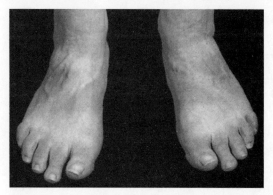

panic. When the storm has passed, she likes to forget and deny it ever happened.

The left ether-toe has a very broad root and tapers gradually. A lot of things that want to be expressed at first go wrong in Barbara's life. What remains is dreaming about how things might have been, because the tip of the toe is somewhat turned up. It is not in touch with the ground. When you push this tip down it immediately lifts itself up. In Barbara's life there is much room for fantasizing. The emotion-toe is tilted towards the ether. There is a clear need to express everything that has to do with emotions. The tip of the emotion-toe is spatula-shaped (she doesn't put a brake on emotions). Yet the shape of the last phalanx shows that there is doubt whether to make contact with the ether or the creativity. The toe is slightly tilted towards the ether, while the tip of the toe is looking for ways to stir up all kinds of creative matters. This is because the tip shows an asymmetry towards creativity. The creativity-toe stands somewhat apart from the emotion-toe. Action will therefore always be put off for a while. Not for very long, but for some time surely (the space between the toes is too small to be called a gap). The creativity-toe can be manipulated and is big and straight. There is a big drop under the toe. There is much more creativity than Barbara actually shows the outside world. It is possible for her to have made something beautiful without anyone knowing that she was ever working on it. The love-toe is directed straight down, into the ground. It is also static and a far cry from the flexibility of the attachment-toe on the right foot. This pattern leads me to believe that in the past a large amount of love was blocked by people close to her. Her passion for singing and dancing, for instance, was nipped in the bud. "Behave yourself" or "Don't make a fuss" are phrases often quoted when such a pattern is found in the love-toe. The trust-toe comes to a point, is not in contact with the ground and has its base close to the love-toe. This means that Barbara draws her trust from her own feelings of love, and doesn't take it from what is offered from the outside. She only trusts herself in that respect. God and other people have given her little reason for optimistic behaviour as far as she is concerned. "When it all comes down to it, you're on your own" could be her motto. Due to this "trusting only herself", her sex life plays a minimal part. Sometimes it is very intense (pointy toe) but then it simmers for a long time.

REASON

Doubtful expression
after reflection

Some reserve concerning
strong desires

Very decisive

Strong attachment

Prone to fear

EMOTIONS

Expressing feelings with
an element of fantasy

Talking and doing
based on feelings

A lot of restrained
creativity

Love blockage

Self-confidence

BARBARA
36 YEARS

Peter – Male – 21 Years

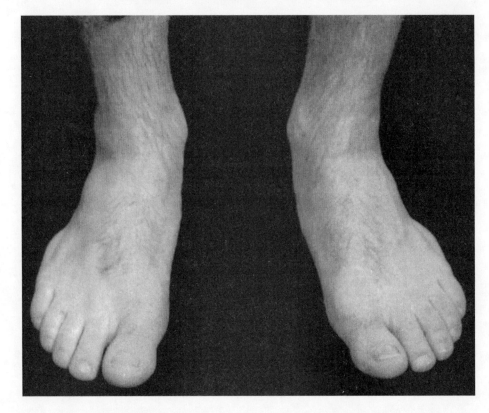

PETER
21 YEARS

RIGHT	LEFT
Big rounded ether-toe not completely earthed	Big rounded ether-toe not completely earthed
Very straight wish-toe angular with round tip	Straight emotion-toe which can hardly be manipulated
Straight activity-toe	Big, flexible creativity-toe
Attachment-toe looks back	Clawing, backward-looking love-toe
Clawing and hiding fear-toe	Clawing and hiding trust-toe

Peter's toes make a balanced, orderly and friendly impression. His ether-toes have the right proportion in comparison with the other toes. Together they give a stable image. His emotional life is a bit bumpy though. This shows in the horizontal ripple-marks on the nails of both big toes. From the broadened sides of both Peter's feet one could derive that he has quite a big potential of earthly energy, but that this energy has not yet developed.

The right ether-toe is big. Peter can speak for himself. When he talks his story grows, and so does his enthusiasm. This is not always justified. Peter can give in to fantasies and daydreaming. The tips of both big toes are not completely earthed. This means that his statements sometimes literally lack a firm foundation. Both ether-toes can be put into the air at an angle of almost 90 degrees. If he wants to, Peter can escape reality and withdraw into a fantasy in which he is completely in control. External influences which have a negative effect in his life can be eliminated. The rounded tip tells us he is a friendly guy, and that he takes other people into considera-tion. He downright loathes confrontations. The wish-toe, being straight and having a rounded tip, tells us that Peter's word is law. Peter won't budge, but he will try to consider other people. The activity-toe offers the same stable image as the wish-toe. Both toes cooperate closely, and we can therefore conclude that his thinking and acting are closely related. Most of the time Peter will start putting his ideas into practice before they have been fully thought out. The attachment-toe shows us that saying goodbye, losing or letting go are difficult for Peter. On top of that he tends to look back. This can lead him to dream about how things would have been if there hadn't been any losses. Preoccupation with thoughts like that can lead to a loss of energy sometimes, and it is then possible that a development is delayed. The little toe, the fear-toe, shows that Peter would rather deal with feelings of agitation and fear in silence, and that they are often gladly flushed down the drain.

The left ether-toe is big, round, and, just like his colleague from the right, "ready for take-off". Peter fantasizes daily. The outside world may consider his remarks about emotional matters as lacking foundation some-times. However, when Peter translates his emotions into action, suddenly, there is understanding. Peter is better at putting his feelings into action than in talking about them. Yet his big ether-toe shows that he cannot stop talk-ing about his feelings. The emotion-toe is straight and can hardly be manip-ulated at all. Although Peter would like to, he can't switch off his feelings. The creativity-toe, however, can be manipulated. It is big and therefore a lot of work can be done, as long as it is stimulated by emotions. Emotions

♂

PETER

21 YEARS

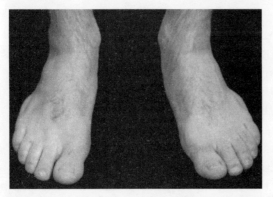

and creativity make a close couple, just like the wish and activity toes on the right foot. The love-toe is a retro-toe, again, like the attachment toe on the right foot. It is therefore quite possible to hear him say that dreaming about love, especially in the past, is far more enjoyable than the real thing. Reality is often disappointing. There is no concrete love. It is not given, and it is not offered either. What really remains from the experience of love does not match the image of earlier fantasies, and Peter prefers not to address this. Down the drain with it then. The toe eventually bends towards the earth. The trust-toe shows that there is trust and optimism in peaks. This also goes for sex. The toe is fierce and pointy, the experience fierce and intense. The outside world, however, should barely notice anything of this. Hide the energy, and therefore the toe.

The broadened outsides of Peter's feet indicate that there is far more earthly energy present than is reflected in the little toes. It is held on to before it can manifest itself in these toes. What this leads to can be unpredictable. You sometimes see that this kind of bottling-up can cause physical complaints. In this case they might emerge in the lowest chakra, in the groin.

REASON

Great, imaginative verbal
ability

Strong-willed

Thinking and acting
closely linked

Very strong attachment

Rejection of fear

EMOTIONS

Expression of feelings
if possible linked to action

Feelings very essential

A lot of creativity
nourished by emotions

Love shortages

Trust and sex in very
strong peaks

♀

PETER

21 YEARS

57

Hannah – Female – 31 Years

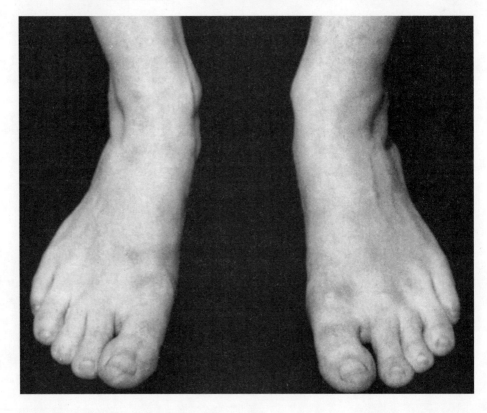

RIGHT	LEFT
Very big ether-toe more moderate in size at the root Slight tilt at tip	Slightly less big ether-toe
Straight wish-toe in full contact with the ground Contact between ether-toe and wish-toe	No contact between emotion-toe and ether-toe Flexible emotion-toe with drop, coming to a spatula shape
Activity-toe and wish-toe basically same shape	Strong kinship between creativity-toe and emotion-toe
Clawing attachment-toe	Big clawing love-toe with twist
Clawing fear-toe	Little trust-toe with big drop

The extremely large big toes dominate the picture at first. There is a large enough verbal ability. Hannah has a big ether and enough room to express herself.

The right ether-toe is moderately sized at the root. This toe grows broader when it literally tries to get in touch with the other toes by tilting a bit. The tip comes to a point and has a round shape. Being round, this toe oozes tact and kindness. The pointy tip means that there is a larger potential than can really be expressed. People with large big toes can often chatter for hours. In this case the pointy tip is probably a concession to the outside world, for everybody would go utterly mad if everything Hannah thought was actually spoken. The big toe also shows an inclination to hurry because it tries to get in touch with the wish-toe. The wish-toe is straight and in full contact with the ground. Hannah knows what she wants. Her activity-toe looks to have grown together with the wish-toe at the root. They make a beautiful couple, which brings thinking and acting into line. An idea is immediately put into action. The attachment-toe has a lot of energy in its last phalanx. This may be inopportune, so the energy flows into the ground (clawing toe). It hurts Hannah initially to lose something, or to let go. She doesn't want to talk about it, however. The more the energy crystallizes, i.e. grows more earthly, the less she'll be prepared to talk about it. The fear-toe is completely bent towards the earth, and hides on top of that. Fear? Don't talk about it, act as if it isn't there. That is her attitude.

♀

HANNAH

31 YEARS

The left ether-toe mainly shows the same pattern as the big toe on the right foot. However, this one is slightly less big. Expressing feelings is somewhat more difficult than talking about the products of her reason. Because she lacks a clear connection with the emotion-toe she can only talk about her feelings at a remove.

Then there is a pattern like: Let me tell you...or should I...Yes, I will...or should I ease up and polish my statements so that I don't step on anybody's toes. When emotions are expressed, they are accompanied by a lot of insecurity and much ado. The emotion-toe can be manipulated but does come to a spatula shape with a drop looking for energy from the creativity. Something must be done with the emotions. As on the right foot, two toes are particularly close together on this foot too. The creativity-toe is married to the emotion-toe. Hannah herself cannot decide which energy is active, the emotion or the creativity. To outsiders this is also not very clear. The explicitly large love-toe is twisted so that it can nurture the creativity. Because love is a water energy, it might temper this creativity,

59

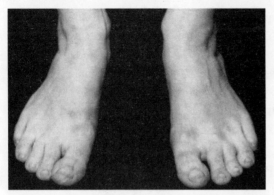

which works so closely together with the emotions, to a large extent. The pattern of the love-toe indicates that when the love energy is active, the love expands. The somewhat clawing tip of this toe indicates that when love is expressed, a part of it flows into the earth. The trust-toe is small. At first glance there is little energy in this toe. Under it, however, there is a big drop. This drop tells us that there is enough trust and optimism from which energy can be drawn quietly. This trust, however, is not radiated. As far as sex is concerned: somewhat out of order, and definitely not something to talk about.

♀

HANNAH
31 YEARS

REASON

Great verbal ability

Purposeful

Decisive

Strong attachment

Denial of fear

EMOTIONS

Hesitant and difficult
expression of feelings

Insecure, yet willing
to express

Creativity and emotions
inseparable

A lot of love energy
expressed hesitantly

Enough trust and
optimism
Restrained sexuality

♀

HANNAH

31 YEARS

Matthew– Male – 3½ Years

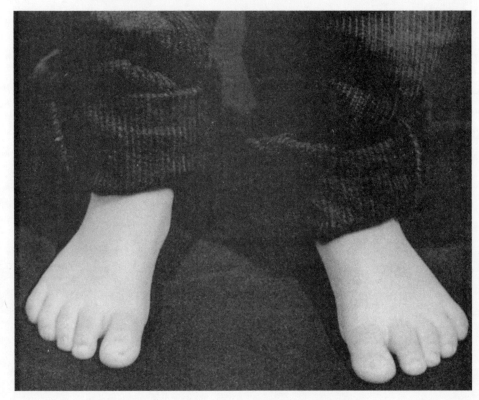

RIGHT	LEFT
Big ether-toe with round tip	Big ether-toe with round tip
Flexible wish-toe with big root and round tip	Flexible, broad emotion-toe with narrower tip
Flexible activity-toe	Creativity-toe with twist
Big attachment-toe looking back	Love-toe looking back
Not earthed fear-toe	Twisted trust-toe not earthed at the base

Both feet show practically the same pattern. His rational and emotional actions are therefore in balance. As you can see, there is a gap between his big toes and the others. Matthew never gives you an instant reaction. He will only show if he likes or dislikes something afterwards. He is a dreamer, but he does have a personality of his own. His broad little feet stand firmly on the ground. You don't push him over easily. He is clearly present.

His right ether-toe is big. He can say everything that comes to mind. It only takes a while because of the gap between the ether-toe and the wish-toe. He is a stable and diplomatic boy. Stable because the toe hardly changes its shape "on the way" and diplomatic because the tip of the toe is round. The wish-toe is stiff at the root and can be manipulated further on. At the end the toe becomes somewhat smaller in size and the tip is round. At first Matthew can be hard to please, but afterwards it isn't so bad. When something can't be carried through, it won't leave him a damaged soul. After all his wish-toe can very well be manipulated. Matthew springs into action especially when he wants something. The activity-toe is closely linked with the wish-toe. His activity-toe can be manipulated too, which means that Matthew can postpone his urge for gratification when it is necessary. The drop under the activity-toe, however, indicates that postponing action indefinitely is out of the question. The restrained fire energy, the drive, is stored in the drop. When Matthew has to wait too long, you can expect an explosion of irritation or even anger. The attachment-toe is big, and turns back very strongly. When a person looks back to that extent, at that age, it almost certainly has to be congenital. Matthew will undoubtedly have troubles with his attachment. When something is taken from him he will react strongly, he will not forget this "injustice" and be vindictive about it for quite a long time. The fear-toe shows that Matthew doesn't know how to deal with fear. There is no reason to be fearful. This toe doesn't touch the ground at all. The toe is tilted so that it touches the attachment-toe. This indicates that Matthew gets scared when he loses something. Losing something leads him to panic. He can even get hysterical when, actually, there isn't any reason to be. A parental divorce, which was not experienced consciously, can produce a similar configuration in children's toes.

The left ether-toe is big and friendly because of the round tip. Like the one on the right foot we can see a gap between the ether and the other energies that have to be brought into ether. However, Matthew will show his feelings at times when those around him don't expect it. He does this with an intensity that doesn't imply that he had "held his water" for a while. The emotion-toe is very broad and can be manipulated. Its end is

♂

MATTHEW

3½ YEARS

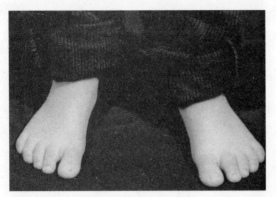

somewhat less broad than indicated by the root. On first acquaintance Matthew seems to be a boy with a lot of feelings. Later on there turn out to be fewer than expected. The combination of manipulation and narrowing often causes Matthew to be indifferent. The creativity-toe is less big than the emotion-toe, and turns towards the emotions. Without emotions there can be no creative actions. The love-toe is a retro-toe which looks for the emotions together with the creativity. Drawing love from the present will be difficult for Matthew in the future. Feelings of love will be drawn from beautiful experiences of the past. His trust-toe shows that such things as positive attitude, trust and sexuality lack any foundation. They will only be accepted when they are nourished with love. The tip of the trust-toe is twisted, so that the entire base makes contact with the love-toe, instead of the earth (as it should).

♂

MATTHEW

3½ YEARS

REASON   EMOTIONS

Stable and diplomatic
expression
No instant reactions

Delayed, intense
expression

Knows what he wants
when is of secondary
importance

A lot of emotions
varyingly expressed,
sometimes even
indifferently

Very strong attachment

Feeling and acting
go closely together

MATTHEW

3½ YEARS

Fears only losing
somebody or something

Love mainly based on
past experiences

Trust based on love

Henrietta– Female – 33 Years

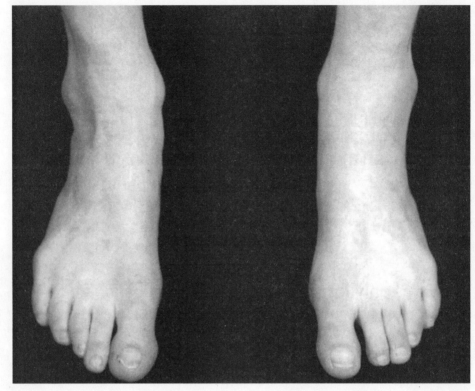

RIGHT	**LEFT**
Right ether-toe with considerable bottleneck and round tip	Left ether-toe with smaller bottleneck less swollen with bigger nail
Wish-toe with bunion	Slightly clawing emotion-toe
Clawing activity-toe hiding under wish-toe	Creativity-toe has parallels with the emotion-toe Broader tip
Attachment-toe with tip pointing to activity-toe	
Fear-toe hiding under attachment-toe	Love-toe not straight and hiding Trust-toe not straight and hiding

The nails of both Henrietta's big toes show regular ripple-marks. In the picture they can hardly be seen, by the way. They indicate that her emotional life isn't very stable. A bumpy emotional life, especially in this period, is my conclusion.

The right ether-toe has a remarkable bottleneck. Expressing her thoughts is not very easy at first. There is some restraint, but then the toe becomes broader. Apparently Henrietta doesn't want to be overlooked, so she decides to express her energy "parked" (restrained) in the bottleneck to the full, after all. The outside world, thinking her a shy little person, is surprised by so much determination in the end. Henrietta herself is then a bit startled by it and modifies her conversation and her remarks to take the sting out of them. In the end all her statements are polished and emollient. Because of the bottleneck shape of the ether toe there is no full contact with the wish-toe. Only a little bit of her material desires can be expressed primarily. At a secondary level, all her desires can be expressed, when a detour leads the energy to the ether via the root of the big toe. The wish-toe is straight with a little bunion on the last phalanx. We can assume that Henrietta thinks she is more pretentious than she considers appropriate. Still she quietly goes her own way. Because the activity-toe doesn't show a straight, harmonious image, it will be difficult for her to put her wishes into practice. The activity-toe does look for the wish-toe, however, and hides partly under it. By doing so it allows the wish-toe to push it against the ground, flushing the activity energy down the drain. This reinforces the impression that the owner absolutely wants to go her way, even secretly.

Henrietta often fails to get what she wants, however. On top of that the activity-toe can be manipulated. The attachment-toe is a real retro-toe as well. It is very difficult to detach herself from material or mental attainments she has gained with much effort. The fear-toe appears to be bigger on closer inspection. It hides under the attachment-toe. This toe also looks back. This leads us to conclude that feelings of fear are derived from the past.

The left foot is another story entirely. The left ether-toe is very open for her energy, after hesitating initially (bottleneck). Yet there is less energy than in the right big toe. This one is less big. The nail is bigger, more in proportion with the toe itself, and the tip is somewhat more angular than that of the right colleague. That is why Henrietta doesn't have any trouble expressing her feelings. Still, everything happening in her emotional life will be expressed "at staggered intervals". The gap, the space between the big toe and the rest of the toes, is a reflection of the way Henrietta only

♀

HENRIETTA

33 YEARS

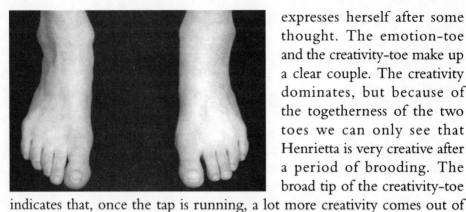

expresses herself after some thought. The emotion-toe and the creativity-toe make up a clear couple. The creativity dominates, but because of the togetherness of the two toes we can only see that Henrietta is very creative after a period of brooding. The broad tip of the creativity-toe indicates that, once the tap is running, a lot more creativity comes out of her than one would expect of such a shy woman. The love-toe has a frustrated position. It hides somewhat under the creativity-toe and looks back. Owners of love-toes like that are inclined to say that in the past, as they recall it, their love life was a bit better. There is also something wrong with the pattern of trust, optimism and sexuality reflected in the little toe. The trust-toe also hides for a large part and looks back. The two smallest toes on both feet show pressure on the energy from the two lowest chakras. This would, projected onto the corresponding areas of the body, indicate problems in the abdomen and the groin. That's where, according to similar patterns in the toes, the body energy cannot flow freely.

♀

HENRIETTA

33 YEARS

REASON

EMOTIONS

Reserved at first

Less trouble with delayed
airing of feelings

Desires in spite
of opposition

Emotions and creativity
clearly linked

Waste of energy

A lot of energy after
a period of brooding

Strong attachment

Love frustration

♀

Fears from the past

Little trust and optimism

HENRIETTA

33 YEARS

Michael – Male – 39 Years

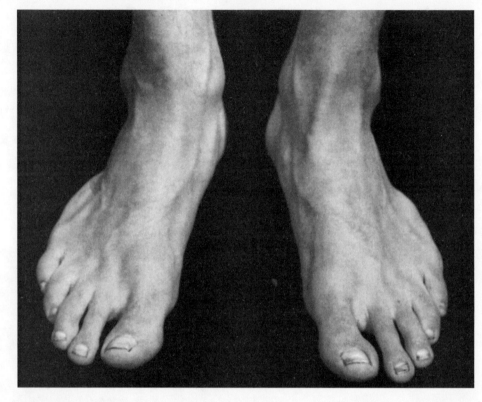

RIGHT	LEFT
Slightly twisted, rounded ether-toe with bottleneck	Block-shaped and rounded ether-toe with broad tip
Narrow wish-toe, ending in block shape	Both spatula-shaped and block-shaped emotion-toe with broad tip
Twisted activity-toe with drop	Straight creativity-toe
Big attachment-toe hiding under activity-toe Retro-toe	Twisted, backward-looking love-toe
Clawing fear-toe	Tilted trust-toe

Michael always wants to do more than he is capable of and he is always busy doing more than one thing at a time. His ether-toes are too short in relation to his other toes.

The right ether-toe narrows to a bottleneck. Then it becomes broader and has a rounded tip. The last phalanx is twisted towards the wish-toe. Everything that happens in Michael's thinking is brought into the ether after a lot of doubting, carefully at first, then with some force. This is shown in the bottleneck and the broad part of the toe that follows. The tip of this toe then becomes pointy and ends round. This indicates a bit of easing up and a way of putting things so that nobody gets worked up about it. The twist in the last phalanx indicates that Michael is not happy about the gap between his big toe and his other toes. Because of this gap there is a delay before all rational expressions are brought into the ether. The toe tries to make contact with the wish-toe in order to narrow the gap and to make it possible for him to react more quickly. There is a change going on which will lead Michael to express himself more directly. The wish-toe is narrow, and looks more moderate. The tip, however, tells us another story. The last phalanx has a block shape. It indicates that there is no budging Michael when he has decided that something must be done. Wishes, initially presented in a moderate manner, are eventually put on the table with a bang. The block shape tells us: "It would take an army to make me budge an inch!!" The activity-toe twists in order to make contact with the wish-toe and by doing so it narrows the gap at the base. Under the last phalanx there is a big drop. Michael places all his fire energy at the service of the block shape on the wish-toe. At first Michael heads straight for the realization of his wishes. But during the process a part of the created fire energy is flushed down the drain. Michael doesn't give himself time to realize his powerfully-felt wishes at a normal pace. The hurry creates more energy in the activity-toe than can possibly be handled. It is then stored in the reservoir, the drop under the toe. Not being able to handle the energy leads to aggression. Michael will often come into conflict with people who try to slow him down. Bureaucracy and red tape will make him furious. Letting go or saying goodbye to all he loves doesn't come easily to him. He attaches himself very strongly to things and people, but he doesn't want to talk or even think about that. That is the story the attachment-toe tells us by being fairly big, and hiding as much as possible. On top of that it is a retro-toe. This means, although Michael won't admit or even deny it, that he is introspective. The fear-toe shows that Michael would very much like to eliminate that emotion. Feelings of fear and unease should not exist, so

♂

MICHAEL

39 YEARS

71

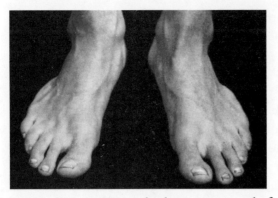

flush them down the drain and don't talk about them.

The emotional side of Michael is less hasty but, in the long run, is presented graphically. The left ether-toe gradually becomes broader and almost shows a block shape at the tip, the rough edges of which are turned.

♂

MICHAEL

39 YEARS

Michael's emotions, which are expressed after some time (gap between the emotions and the ether), are put down on the table emphatically. You can't ignore them. It is not his intention to dominate others with his emotions, but they have to be expressed fully. The emotion-toe shows a pattern of hesitating somewhat. Then the toe becomes broader. Because of this a two-lane highway is put at the disposal of the emotions, as it were. When the emotional energy is active, it gradually builds up to a compromise between a spatula shape and a block shape. The creativity-toe is straight and stable. It works closely together with the emotion-toe, a strong couple that can manage quite a lot together. Because of the gap between the ether toe and the others it takes some time before creative manifestations become apparent. The love-toe tells us that love can best be put into the creativity. Despite the fact that the water energy might put out the fire energy of the creativity-toe, the creativity-toe doesn't seem to be bothered by that in the slightest. The love-toe looks back and places itself at the service of creative processes. This sometimes leads to conflicts with the outside world, which receives little love from Michael. Practically all his love is put into his own activities. The trust-toe is tilted and not very big. Every energy developed in the groin is presented a little differently from the way they are dealt with by Michael himself. Michael will even deny the possible religious basis of his trust and optimism, even though there is a little present of both elements.

REASON   EMOTIONS

REASON	EMOTIONS
Changing, hesitating expression	Emphatic expressing of emotions
Unshakeable desires	Emotions and creativity closely linked
Acting too hastily	Strong creativity
trong inner attachment	Love is put into own activities
Denial of fear	Sex and trust presented differently

♂
MICHAEL
39 YEARS

Sarah – Female – 26 Years

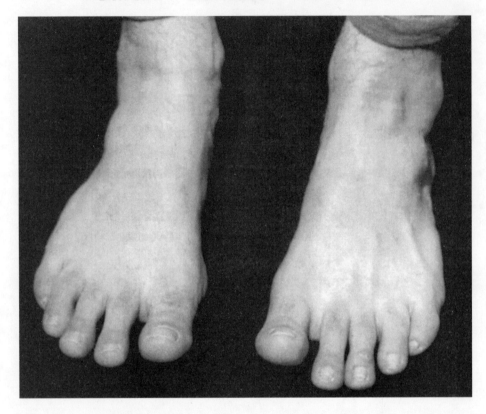

♀

SARAH

26 YEARS

RIGHT	**LEFT**
Round, not earthed ether-toe	Bigger, upturned ether-toe
Broad-based wish-toe with bottleneck and broad tip	Straight, somewhat pinched emotion-toe with asymmetric tip
Flexible activity-toe with bottleneck and broad tip	Creativity-toe with bottleneck and callosity Slightly spatula-shaped
Attachment-toe with drop clawing after first phalanx	Big love-toe with drop
Relatively small fear-toe	Moveable trust-toe coming to a point

There are very big gaps between the ether-toes and the other toes. This indicates delayed acting and reacting. You can never expect a primary re-action from Sarah. When she talks, her conversation will gradually become more elaborate (big toes become broader). Because both ether-toes have round tips we can conclude that Sarah takes other people's feelings into consideration. She will always put things more mildly than she actually intends.

Sarah's right ether-toe stands apart from her wish-toe because of the sizeable gap in between. This reminds us of a chess player who thinks for a long time before she makes a move. On top of that the tip is not earthed because of the tendency to point up a bit. When life rushes Sarah too fast, she can always escape into daydreams and fantasies. The wish-toe is big at the root, is then pinched to a bottleneck and is as broad at its base as at the tip. The tip is rounded. This image reflects: knowing what you want at first, then reflecting for a moment whether it is possible or desired or maybe not, and finally expressing the wish after a delay, because of the gap. The fact that the wish-toe can be manipulated adds to the complication. Taken all in all, this shows that nothing much will come of what Sarah wants. All the more because there is also a gap between the wish-toe and the activity-toe. The activity-toe narrows after the first phalanx, then runs into a clear bottleneck and explodes as it were. This shows that when Sarah does act, she will do something unexpectedly drastic. This on the pretext of: "I have to realize some of my wishes!" The fact that the activity-toe can be manipulated, and that the explosion of activity can be postponed, will lead to pointless anger and aggression directed at everybody and every-thing. The attachment-toe is bent towards the earth after the first phalanx and has a drop at the tip. Even before something has been attained, Sarah will be attached to it. This attachment-toe tries to make contact with the activity-toe and claims results prematurely. Her fear-toe is very small in relation to the other toes. There is little energy in that toe. On top of that the toe hides as well. Sarah hardly ever deals with fear. If unease and fear ever come over her she can always escape in daydreaming.

The left ether-toe is somewhat bigger than its colleague on the right. This is a true upturned toe that couldn't even put its tip on the ground if it wanted to. There is lots and lots of fantasy here. It is not based on rational grounds. It is next to impossible to say which energies are responsible for such a turbulent imagination. The gap between the ether-toe and the emotion-toe is big. Energy flowing to the ether-toe arrives there so late that the matching thought has faded and is then mixed with the fantasy

♀

SARAH

26 YEARS

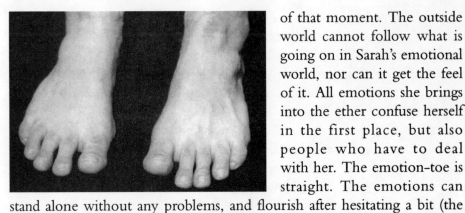

of that moment. The outside world cannot follow what is going on in Sarah's emotional world, nor can it get the feel of it. All emotions she brings into the ether confuse herself in the first place, but also people who have to deal with her. The emotion-toe is straight. The emotions can stand alone without any problems, and flourish after hesitating a bit (the somewhat squeezed second phalanx). Preferably, the emotions are turned into something creative. The detour to the ether is long. That is why this toe has an asymmetric tip with which to look for contact with the creativity-toe. The creativity-toe initially seems to enter into a close alliance with the emotions. The second term brings about hesitation and doubt (bottleneck at the second phalanx). Then (callosity where the toe becomes broader again) it decides to work together with the emotion-toe (towards which it is slightly tilted in a slight spatula shape) as inconspicuously as possible. This rather complicated sequence of yes-no-eventually (when the tips of both toes find each other) leads to unexpectedly neat creative expressions. The love-toe has a big build and a drop to ensure extra grounding. Love is present more emphatically and in larger amounts than can actually be seen (drop). The trust-toe shows that optimism, trust and sexuality are basically strongly present (at the root). In the development of these energies the trust-toe obviously looks out for the love-toe. The trust-toe tries to hide under the love-toe but without success. It can be manipulated better than one would expect. Toe at work! Apparently Sarah is very preoccupied with being more open about her sexual feelings, if only they are nourished with love. Bursts of optimism and trust are better accepted (bursts because of the pointy tip of the little toe).

♀

SARAH

26 YEARS

REASON

EMOTIONS

Strong, delayed reaction

Extensive imagination
leading to confusion

Whimsical

Likes to convert emotions
into creative activity

Explosive

Strong degree of creativity

Possessive

A lot of love present

Little fear

Trust and sex depend on
love
Optimism in bursts

♀

SARAH

26 YEARS

Tony – Male – 34 Years

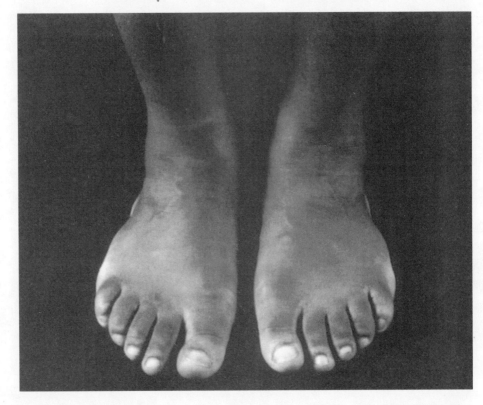

RIGHT	**LEFT**
Round, twisted ether-toe	Round, rushing ether-toe
Large, long wish-toe with round tip can be withdrawn	Long, straight emotion-toe with angular tip can be withdrawn
Stocky activity-toe which can be withdrawn	Round creativity-toe can be withdrawn
Crooked attachment-toe looking back	Sizeable, pointy love-toe looking back
Crooked, pointy fear-toe looking back	Bulky, pointy trust-toe looking back

What immediately catches the eye, when analyzing Tony's toes, is that he can withdraw his second and third toes of both feet quite easily. Also significant is that he is best at expressing his feelings. Dealing with rational matters comes second.

The right ether-toe is round and somewhat twisted. This indicates tact and consideration. The twist indicates that Tony often changes tack while talking. His conversation constantly twists and turns in an effort to appeal more to the listener. The gap between the big toe and the second toe indicates that Tony reacts after a while, rather than immediately, and only then says what he thinks. Tony's wish-toe is longer than the big toe, it is round and withdrawn constantly. This toe shows that Tony occupies himself with more than one issue at a time. He is ambitious, but he will never let his ambition run riot at the cost of others. Tony is very sensitive to what people around him think of his wishes, and should he suspect the merest hint of disapproval, he will 'throttle back'. When the coast is clear, however, he will still do exactly as he intended in the first place. The apparent climbdown was only a smoke-screen. The activity-toe, which is in good contact with the wish-toe, shows that Tony can spring into action easily. Ideas are acted upon without any problems. This toe can be withdrawn as well. This indicates that Tony presents himself as being less active than he really is. He acts in such a way as to make those around him think that he has bowed to the wishes of the outside world. This is purely superficial. After the toe has been withdrawn (reserve) it springs back when the coast is clear (doing what was intended from the outset). The crooked, rather pointy attachment-toe that looks back shows that Tony likes to control and guard what he has achieved. If something is taken from him, this leads to anger and aggression. He stops being the friendly, tactful man he is known to be. Because of the looking back the elements fire (activity-toe) and water (attachment-toe) are confronted with each other and this leads to temper tantrums. The fear-toe is not that large, so there is not a lot of insecurity and fear. Because of the bend the fear is not expressed, but diverted into the ground. Insecurity and fear are preferably not communicated at all.

The left ether-toe is round and has its tip obviously on the ground. Emotions are expressed with ease and in a friendly way. Contrary to the right foot, there is no gap to hamper expression. The left foot has a lump near the big toe which is larger than on the right foot. This indicates that Tony will be more inclined to help if someone tries to convince him with emotional arguments rather than rational ones. Tony's most striking asset in

♂

TONY

34 YEARS

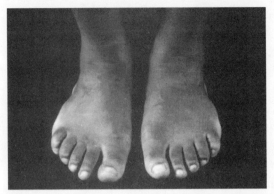

the toe department is the emotion-toe. It is long, almost has a spatula shape, is in good contact with the ground and constantly withdrawn. This toe shows a slight inclination to rush matters because of the asymmetry towards the creativity-toe. Therefore, emotions have to be transformed into creative forms of expression very quickly. The creativity-toe is under pressure from the emotion-toe. Tony creates primarily from his emotions. Yet the emotion-toe is withdrawn regularly and shows that Tony pretends to conform when he suspects that someone close to him thinks he is being too active or when he thinks that the outside world does not appreciate his creative statements. But every time it becomes clear that Tony is unable to restrain his creative energy for long and, just when you think he has throttled back, he will brim over with creativity. The big love-toe leans towards the creativity-toe. A lot of love is incorporated in creative expressions. Because the toe has a somewhat pointy tip, love is expressed sharply in overwhelming amounts. Shortly afterwards, the feelings of love seem to dissipate quickly. Love is only moderately expressed physically. The considerable, crooked and pointy trust-toe curves toward the earth and looks for the love-toe. Tony is confronted with lots of trust and sexual expressions in waves. The left little toe seeks contact with the love-toe, which prevents Tony from having sex without love.

TONY

34 YEARS

80

REASON　　　EMOTIONS

Tactical and considerate

Expresses his feelings
more easily

Wants a lot but does not
always show this

Lots of emotions that will
only be expressed if those
around him let him

Decisiveness is dependent
on the circumstances

Restrains his creativity
should those around him
not accept it

Guards his achievements

Lots of love, mainly in
peaks and expressed in
creativity

Denial of insecurity

Waves of trust and sexual
activity

♂
TONY
34 YEARS

81

Louisa – Female – 39 Years

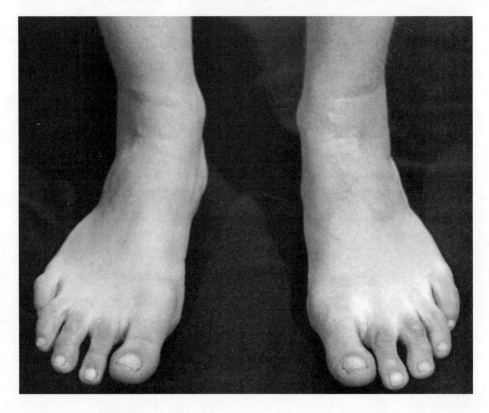

RIGHT	LEFT
Ether-toe with bottleneck with broad, round tip	Slight lump at base of ether-toe
Flexible, broad-rooted wish-toe with some callosity at the base	Broad-rooted emotion-toe with bottleneck and angular tip
Big, clawing activity-toe some callosity at the base	Creativity-toe with callosity on top of first phalanx Clawing at the base Angular tip
Clawing attachment-toe	Love-toe with some callosity and slightly clawing
Clawing fear-toe	Very tense, clawing trust-toe

Louisa's feet reflect so many different kinds of energy that she herself gets confused. It is no wonder that the outside world doesn't get anything out of her. Louisa is in search of her identity. The big roots of her big toes retain a lot of energy, preventing them from developing the way they should. This can cause lumps to form, indicating that Louisa puts up with a lot of things, and that she is inclined to attach more importance to the wishes of other people. Both ether-toes are short in comparison with the other toes. Chaos and disorder are the result. The overall image of the left foot indicates that she camouflages much. This is also shown in the callosities on the air toe and the fire toe.

The right ether-toe has a bottleneck, indicating hesitation. Then the toe becomes broader, indicating renewed determination. Yet she immediately throttles back, tones down and softens the edges of the things she wants to say. The toe has a round tip. The wish-toe, which stands apart, has a broad root with some callosity and little energy. Furthermore, this toe can be manipulated. At first Louisa is hard to please, then she gives up most of her wishes. Things she wants can be postponed or even cancelled as far as she is concerned, although she doesn't like it. All of this under the pretext of: "I've learned that most of what I want, I don't get anyhow." This is correct, for the activity-toe does not remotely join in with the wish-toe. Only after a long detour can she sometimes manage a little decisiveness. At the root of the activity-toe, on top, there is a little callosity. It seems as though Louisa, when she does eventually act, worries that she might be doing the wrong thing. However she has ample fire energy. The activity-toe is bigger than the wish-toe. The fact that these toes have different sizes results in a strained relationship. To compensate for this, the energy leading Louisa to act is drained into the earth because of the clawing shape. Because there is energy with which nothing is done, anger and aggression are the result. The attachment-toe claws towards the ground and flushes all upcoming thoughts convincingly down the drain.

Attachment and the fact that she thinks it unreasonable to let go of anything acquired with great effort are not expressed but flushed down the drain. The fear-toe tells us that fear is denied completely and is drained into the earth as quickly as possible. She can talk about that. At the base of the left ether-toe is quite a reservoir of energy. This indicates a willingness to serve and self-effacement. Louisa is not very good at expressing her feelings yet, but the ether-toe looks out for the emotion-toe and it apparently makes contact with it when the foot spreads out. Their shapes seem to have been "moulded" to each other. If the toe had been as broad as its root, one

♀

LOUISA

39 YEARS

83

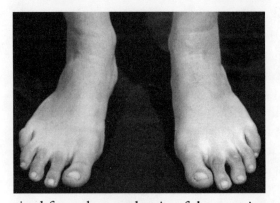

would have been shocked by the amount of emotions. This force is camouflaged by the callosity on the root. Then the emotions stagnate in the bottleneck, but they end by being expressed as broadly and strongly as possible, even dogmatically. This uncompromising attitude can be derived from the angular tip of the emotion-toe. The creativity-toe gives an impression of "not knowing what she wants" and there is doubt, obviously. The big toe is camouflaged by a callosity at first. Then the energy is drained into the earth by the clawing shape. Just before the energy flows into the ground it seems to cooperate better with the emotion-toe, to end up expressing something creative. The tip of the creativity-toe just in time puts itself flat and firmly on the ground. The angular tip of the toe tells us that, now that the time to act has finally come, there will be no fudging or compromises. Nothing must stand in her way. All of her doubt resolves itself in determination. The love-toe does have a little callosity too. Love is therefore eventually hidden from view a little, does not develop very well and is partly drained into the earth, because of the clawing shape of the toe. The trust-toe is very tense. Here is a lot of activity, trying to break out of a pattern. Trust in the future bubbles up and sexual imperatives are on the brink of being admitted and worked out.

♀

LOUISA
39 YEARS

REASON   EMOTIONS

Confused, hesitant expression   Expression of feelings developing

Enforced modesty   A lot of feelings

Big, restrained decisiveness   Expressing creativity hesitantly at first, uncompromisingly later on

Forced independence   Little love-life

Denial of fear   Sexuality and trust developing

LOUISA

39 YEARS

85

Paul – Male – 28 Years

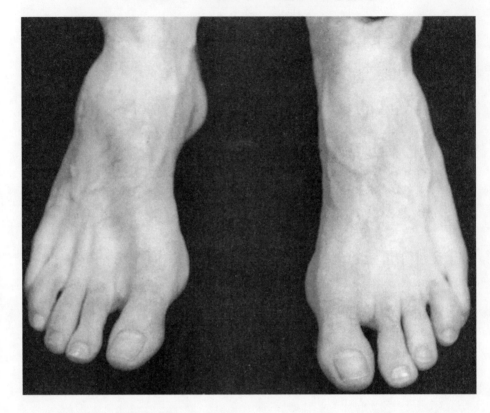

RIGHT	**LEFT**
Ether-toe with lump at base and bottleneck	Big ether-toe with lump at base and bottleneck coming to a point
Wish-toe with slight callosity on first phalanx and bottleneck Straight tip slightly rounded on one side	Broad-tipped, rushing emotion-toe
Big, rounded activity-toe	Stable, straight creativity toe
Clawing attachment-toe	Big, clawing, backward-looking love-toe
Hiding fear-toe	Straight trust-toe

The most striking features of these feet are the lumps at the bases of both ether-toes. Also there is a big gap between the ether-toe and the wish-toe. On the left foot a similar gap is somewhat narrowed. This shows that Paul is a helpful man of feeling who presents himself as a doubter when it concerns rational matters.

The right ether-toe originates from a reservoir, which implies servitude. After the root the toe becomes narrower in a flowing line and forms a bottleneck. Then, again in a flowing line, the toe becomes broader and narrows in the end. This image indicates that Paul is a man who, in flowing wave-like motions, changes from volubility to a guarded silence. In the end, when it all comes down to it, he becomes insecure or modest, and he allows other people to talk first. This "allowing other people to talk first" is shown in the shape of the last phalanx which seems to efface itself gradually. The gap between the wish-toe and the ether-toe shows that rational matters are not brought into the ether immediately. Paul only talks about rational matters reluctantly. The wish-toe is covered by a little callosity at the root. It seems as if Paul is a little embarrassed to express his desires. This is confirmed by the bottleneck which follows the callosity. He throttles back, although he has difficulties doing that. Eventually he brings up his wishes. The wish-toe then tries to assume a block shape, but this is doubted too. On the side of the ether the wishes are smoothed down, rounded off; on the side of the activity-toe there is more certainty. The tip of the toe is straight. This means that, ultimately, Paul's word is law. Paul will take action to fulfil his wishes himself. Talking about them is not in his line. The activity-toe is big in proportion to the wish-toe. Paul has more than enough energy to deal with everything he really wants to do. The well-shaped activity-toe indicates that Paul does this in a stable, balanced way. Paul does see to it, however, that he doesn't hurt people by his actions (the tip is round). The clawing attachment-toe appears to tell us: away with attachment, that is not something to be proud of. That is why Paul prefers not to talk about losses of any kind. The fear-toe is completely hidden. Paul thinks that feelings of fear and unease are not to be talked about at all, as far as he is concerned.

♂

PAUL

28 YEARS

The left ether-toe bears a great resemblance to the one on the right, but it is bigger. To give service, placing himself at the disposal of others, is natural to Paul. He puts emotional arguments before rational ones. The bottleneck and the tip coming to a point reveal the ingrained doubt. The gap between the ether-toe and the wish-toe is smaller than the one on the right foot. Paul expresses his emotions more readily than his rational

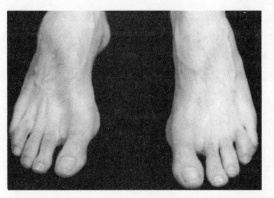

promptings. The emotion-toe grows broader. Emotions developing at the base gradually become stronger. The broad tip seems to turn away from the ether-toe and emphatically looks out for the creativity-toe. It looks as though there once was direct contact with the ether-toe.

This image leads us to suspect that Paul has learned his lesson about expressing his feelings. Now he focuses all his emotions emphatically on creative matters. The emotion-toe is also a rushing toe. There are a lot of emotions, and they have to be converted into creative matters as quickly as possible. The creativity-toe is impeccably straight and appears to be the most stable one in the overall picture. Paul's strength, among others, lies in developing fire energy, in decisiveness. All the more because the air element fans the fire element of the creativity-toe. The love-toe claws and looks back. The love-toe, in itself big and rather long, adjusts itself to the line of the other toes. The potentially present love is flushed down the drain and therefore not developed. This indicates an influence from the outside. Paul paid his dues when he expressed too much love. That hurt and it won't happen again: he would just as soon drain it into the earth, which he does. From the fact that the love-toe turns away from the trust-toe, but that it does look out for contact with the earth, we can gather that Paul's love energy is converted into sexual expressions. The trust-toe is very straight, but is kept out of the picture by the love-toe. There is enough trust and optimism. A very straight trust-toe indicates that someone conducts his sex life smoothly and without frustration. In Paul's case, however, this happens below the surface.

The flows of energy in the two lowest chakras are badly out of kilter with the picture offered by the other toes. We can therefore rightly conclude that when Paul has physical problems, they will occur in the area of the lowest chakras, the abdomen and the groin.

♂

PAUL

28 YEARS

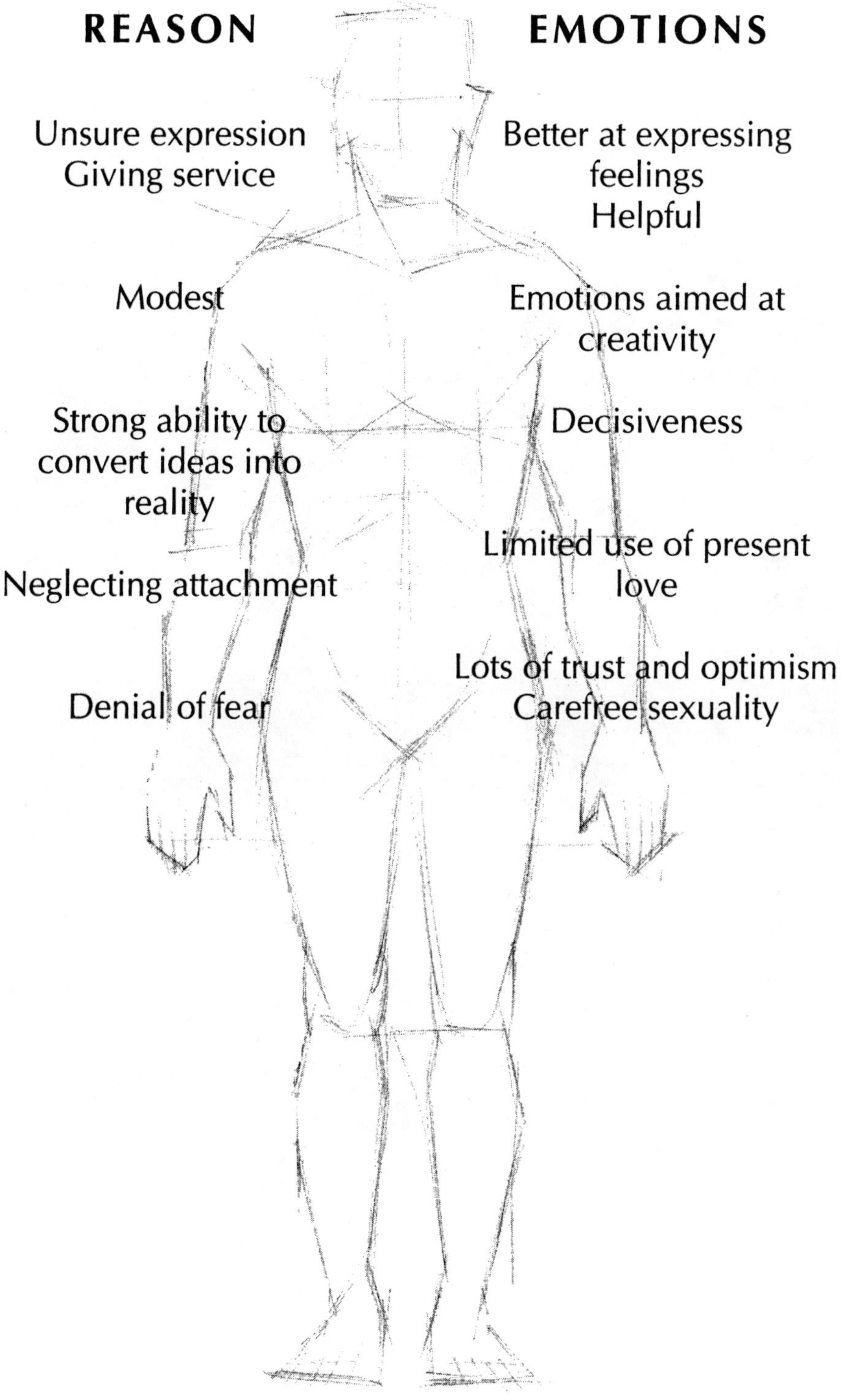

REASON

EMOTIONS

Unsure expression
Giving service

Better at expressing
feelings
Helpful

Modest

Emotions aimed at
creativity

Strong ability to
convert ideas into
reality

Decisiveness

Neglecting attachment

Limited use of present
love

PAUL

28 YEARS

Denial of fear

Lots of trust and optimism
Carefree sexuality

Jacqueline – Female – 42 Years

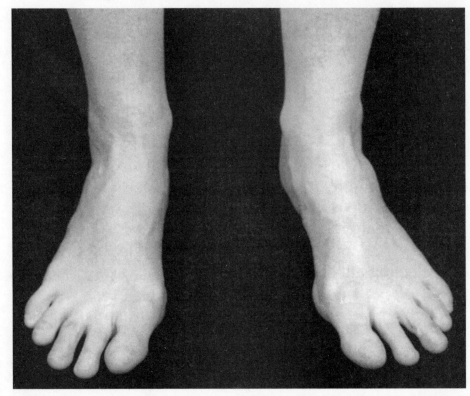

RIGHT	**LEFT**
Twisted, little ether-toe	More straight ether-toe
Straight even wish-toe	Straight emotion-toe
Straight, big flexible activity-toe with callosity	Big, somewhat bumpy creativity-toe
Straight flexible attachment-toe	Love-toe with parallels with creativity-toe
Clawing fear-toe with drop	Trust-toe hiding under love-toe

The toes appear uneven, although several toes are properly straight. There are many gaps between the individual toes. Therefore the most striking feature is the lack of coherence and balance between all energies and corresponding emotions.

The right ether-toe is that of someone who, when it comes down to it, doesn't dare say what she thinks. If she opens her mouth at all, what she says is affected by insecurity. The last phalanx is twisted towards the wish-toe. The big toe is too small in comparison to the other toes. All energies reflected in the other toes will have to "put up a fight" to penetrate the ether. They cannot be expressed all at once. This causes confusion and chaos. The two next toes dominate. This means that these will be brought into the ether most of the time. She will mostly talk about "I want to… and I do…" The wish-toe is straight and well-balanced. Jacqueline does know very well what she wants. Fulfilling her wishes, however, is an entirely different story. The wish energy has to make an encircling movement to reach the fire element of the activity-toe. She doesn't act except after some delay. Jacqueline is not able to act immediately or on impulse. The activity-toe is very straight too, and somewhat bigger than the wish-toe. This indicates quite a lot of aggression. The callosity on the activity-toe reveals that she prefers to hide this aggression. This toe too stands somewhat isolated and has no direct contact with the fellow toes. To outsiders it will never be completely clear what makes Jacqueline angry. Because there is no sideways toe-contact, a postponed expression of irritation can erupt for no reason weeks later. She will express it, no matter how long after the initial provocation. This right fire toe is as straight as an arrow. Even though it can be manipulated: the energy comes out, no matter how! The attachment-toe is straight and somewhat small compared with the wish-toe and the activity-toe. Jacqueline deals with this emotion in a normal fashion and she is even quite capable of handling her attachments. The fear-toe shows that there is no place for this emotion. Drain it. On closer inspection there is a big drop under this toe. That drop indicates that there is a lot of fear present, although she won't express it openly. Jacqueline will deny ever being afraid, and put on the "won't be so bad" act.

The left foot shows a pattern of "not being able to join in". The left ether-toe is not very big, but nonetheless straighter than the other ether-toe. What we have here is a woman with delayed reactions, careful not to hurt or annoy others. This delay is because there is a gap between the emotion-toe and the ether. The emotion-toe is a beautifully straight toe.

♀

JACQUELINE

42 YEARS

91

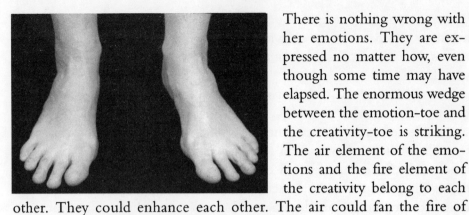

There is nothing wrong with her emotions. They are expressed no matter how, even though some time may have elapsed. The enormous wedge between the emotion-toe and the creativity-toe is striking. The air element of the emotions and the fire element of the creativity belong to each other. They could enhance each other. The air could fan the fire of creativity. But that is not the case here. The fire element is put out by the water element of the love-toe. Possibly to temper the excess of individual creativity a little. The creativity-toe is very big in proportion to the other toes. So there is a lot of creative energy. The toe is a bit bumpy. It looks as if it has had to deal with some collisions in the process of developing, and has come out the worse for wear. The creativity which, because of the toe's straight shape is expressed no matter what, is not always appreciated. The love-toe works together with the creativity-toe. This is rather unusual but, as I have already stated, this cooperation can have a tempering result. The trust-toe hides under its neighbour. Optimism and trust hide under love. Nothing much will come of dealing with sexuality, and when Jacqueline tries to deal with it, this will be a direct result of love and it will be dealt with in silence.

JACQUELINE
42 YEARS

REASON   EMOTIONS

Careful, sometimes   Expressing emotions after
muddled, expression   reflection without hurting
                            feelings

Considered acts   Well-ordered emotions

Restrained aggression   A lot of creative
expressed after delay   energy

Normal attachment   Love and creativity
                            closely linked

Denial of fear   Optimism and trust
                            dependent on love

♀

JACQUELINE

42 YEARS

93

Leo – Male – 32 Years

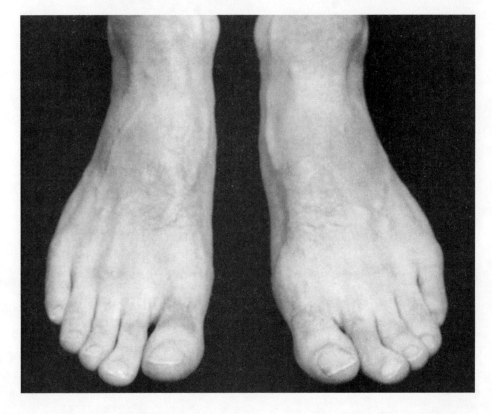

RIGHT	LEFT
Broadening ether-toe with narrow base	Somewhat tapering twisted ether-toe with round tip
Somewhat tapering with round tip	
Hurrying, big, flexible wish-toe	Emotion-toe with much hurrying impatience
Asymmetric spatula shape	
Flexible wish-toe	Big, flexible creativity-toe
Big and straight attachment-toe	Straight love-toe
Relatively small, somewhat hiding fear-toe	Clawing and hiding trust-toe
Retro-toe	

The most striking features at first glance are the somewhat small ether-toes and hurrying, impatient second toes. Both ether-toes can be put in the air at an angle of almost ninety degrees while the other toes remain firmly on the ground. The ability to do this indicates that Leo can escape reality and "surrender himself to daydreaming" very well.

The right ether-toe is narrow at the root and then becomes broader. The tip tapers a bit and has a round end (friendly and tactful). At first, the owner of these toes doesn't have a lot to say. Leo once used to put his thoughts into words only after reflection (there was a gap between the ether-toe and the wish-toe). This original pattern of behaviour has changed through the years. He has learned to talk mainly of his intentions. Initially he seems to do this somewhat shyly, somewhat reservedly (narrow at the root), but when he is talking, his conversation becomes ever more enthusiastic. It looks as though Leo wants to convince himself by talking long and enthusiastically about his plans. Most of the time he will also develop and work out his plans while talking. The wish-toe is big. Leo wants a lot. The last phalanx has an asymmetric spatula shape. This is a real rush-toe. On top of that this toe can be manipulated. Wishes can be deferred for a while. This toe touches the ether-toe before the last phalanx. This means that his wishes are brought into the ether before they are worked out and reflected on. Leo habitually makes premature statements. Talking about his plans does help him, however. He puts pressure on himself by giving the impression that he is further along with them than he actually is. He constantly does this. The activity-toe is subject to pressure by the wish-toe. This toe pushes its tip to the right. Because of this the toe cannot grow straight and has to behave like a rush-toe under pressure. This activity-toe can be manipulated, which often happens. Its shape indicates that it is withdrawn regularly. Postponing action is something Leo does constantly. Leo has many wishes, and he talks about them a lot, arousing many expectations. To meet them, he would have to work every moment of the day. But before one job had been taken care of, the others would be piling up. The result is chaos. The activity-toe shows that in such cases, he throttles back for a while and he marks time. Leo brakes, works out his priorities and then steps on the gas. Attachment is present in large quantities. The attachment-toe is big and straight. "All that I have attained is mine" is what this toe seems to tell us. But when he has to let go of something, this causes no problems. There are so many wishes and there is so much "toe at work", that there will always be a substitute. The fear-toe is not very big in relation to the other toes. It hides a little. This earth-toe doesn't contain a lot of

♂
LEO
32 YEARS

95

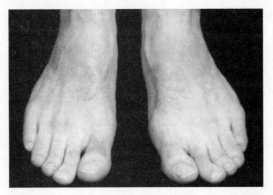

ether energy. With such a pattern you have to interpret fear as unease. From the fact that this toe "looks back" and seeks contact with the attachment-toe, you can deduce that when Leo has to let go of something, he will become agitated.

The left ether-toe shows the same pattern as the right one, but the tip is a little more pointy. Expressing his emotions becomes gradually more easy for Leo. When he brings something into the ether, he does this in a friendly and amiable way, but slightly differently than is experienced by his inner self (twist). The ether-toe has good contact with the emotion-toe. This gives us the idea that Leo immediately expresses everything he feels. This is only partly true. The emotion-toe is very revealing. This toe is as straight as an arrow as long as it is in touch with the ether-toe. Before the emotions have developed completely, it is easy for Leo to talk about them. When it all comes down to it, however, he chooses not to talk, but to convert his emotions into decisiveness. Leo thinks that, as far as his emotional life is concerned, he has been shortchanged. Being in love will be overwhelming for Leo at first. A typical case of "biting off more than he can chew". Just as on the right foot, the fire energy is under pressure. There is still more of it here. The creativity-toe has a larger shape, and makes a "more certain" impression than the activity-toe. It can be manipulated and Leo can therefore easily put up with some delay in carrying out his creativity. The love-toe is straight and trampled underfoot a bit as it were by the creativity-toe which, under pressure of the emotion-toe, has an emergency too. This causes the stable handling of love to remain out of the picture a little. Yet Leo is steady and trustworthy in all that he loves. The trust-toe creeps entirely towards the love-toe, and is therefore nearly invisible. Leo hardly talks about what happens with the earth energy in his left foot if he talks about it at all. He will only show the ones he loves very much what he feels there.

REASON

EMOTIONS

Expressing a lot and
lengthily

Expressing friendly but
reserved, and different
from the way he
experiences it himself

A lot of wishes

Prefers to convert
emotions into
decisiveness

A variability in his
capacity for realizing
plans

Creativity under pressure

LEO

32 YEARS

Big attachment

Steady and trustworthy
love partner

Unease

Trust and sex expressed
indirectly and selectively

97

Charlotte – Female – 7 Years

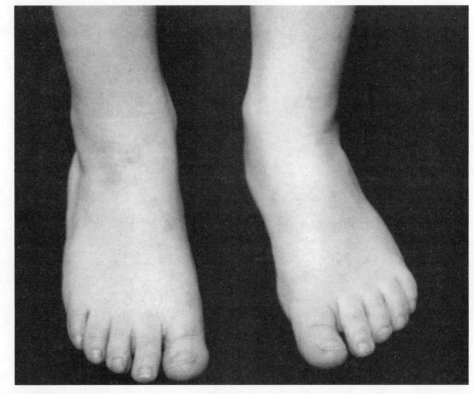

RIGHT	LEFT
Ether-toe with upturned tip Rush-toe	Smaller ether-toe with upturned tip and rush
Rushing wish-toe	Static emotion-toe
Flexible activity-toe with drop	Creativity-toe with drop
Straight, flexible attachment-toe	Clawing love-toe
Pointy, hiding fear-toe	Hiding, supple trust-toe

Charlotte's big toes attract attention immediately. Both toes are dream-toes and both of them are twisted. When you ask her to keep all toes on the ground, and raise her big toes at a ninety-degree angle, she turns out to be able to do that. Charlotte is a dreamer. She lives in her own little world. She fantasizes and constantly reinterprets reality in her own way. Because of her ability to raise her big toes from the ground she can escape reality completely. She doesn't have a lot of feeling for the reality of life.

The right ether-toe is in a hurry because of the twist. This means that Charlotte talks a lot and fast. The round tip of this big ether-toe shows that she is a sweet little girl who won't hurt or harm anybody. There is a little space between the ether-toe and the wish-toe. That is because the wish-toe, just like the ether-toe, is a rush-toe. Charlotte would like to see her wishes fulfilled quickly and she doubts time and time again whether to go into action herself, or to ask somebody to help her. This can be derived from the isolated position of the wish-toe. Under the activity-toe Charlotte has a big drop. When the energy stored in there is set free, Charlotte can manage a good tantrum. Charlotte gets angry when what she wants doesn't happen. The wish-toe is in a hurry, but is not able to join in with the activity-toe. After all, the fire energy is needed to translate her wishes into actions. This lack of coordination leads to aggravation and even to anger (because of the big drop). However, the expression of anger can be postponed a little, because the toe can also be manipulated. Apparently, Charlotte has already learned that there is no point in getting angry at any old time. You have to wait until someone is nearby to aim your anger at. The time of sitting-alone-in-a-corner-being-angry is behind her. The attachment-toe can be manipulated as well. This doesn't lead to any troubles. On the contrary. Because the pattern is beautifully straight, we may assume that Charlotte can miss something. The fear-toe hides and comes to a point. She doesn't want to be afraid, but she is sometimes, even very much for a short while.

The big toe on the left foot, the left ether-toe, is clearly smaller than the one on the right foot. There is little sorrow, but a little ether as well. Expressing rational matters will come more easily to her than talking about her emotional life. There is a little gap between the ether-toe and the emotion-toe too. Some time passes before Charlotte informs others of her feelings. The emotion-toe can't be manipulated. So she can't "fiddle" with her feelings. What Charlotte feels, she feels. When the outside world doesn't accept that, the toe will claw eventually, because it can't be manipulated. There is enough energy in the creativity-toe. Here too, just like in the right

♀

CHARLOTTE

7 YEARS

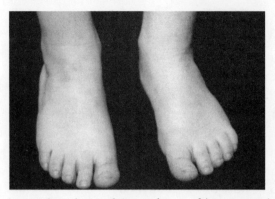

fire-toe, there's a drop. There is more creativity present than meets the eye. When the creativity can join in with the rich imagination by way of the emotions, Charlotte might very well become a successful artist. Her love-toe flushes some down the drain already. Love is not expressed, but either drained (into the earth) or experienced introvertly. The trust-toe on the left foot shows that optimism and trust are under pressure. The little toe may be hiding, but it is still very supple. It is essential for Charlotte's further development for her to learn that trusting in people and the future is worthwhile. If she doesn't, she will have problems with love and expressing it for the rest of her life. In that case she will regularly withdraw into her imagination. This can lead to solitude and isolation.

♀

CHARLOTTE

7 YEARS

REASON

EMOTIONS

Talking fast and much

Delayed and more difficult expression of emotions

Varying initiative

No restriction concerning own emotions

Wishes often not translated into action
Anger because of this

A lot of creativity

Not possessive

Introverted concerning love and affection

Fear in peaks

Varying degrees of trust

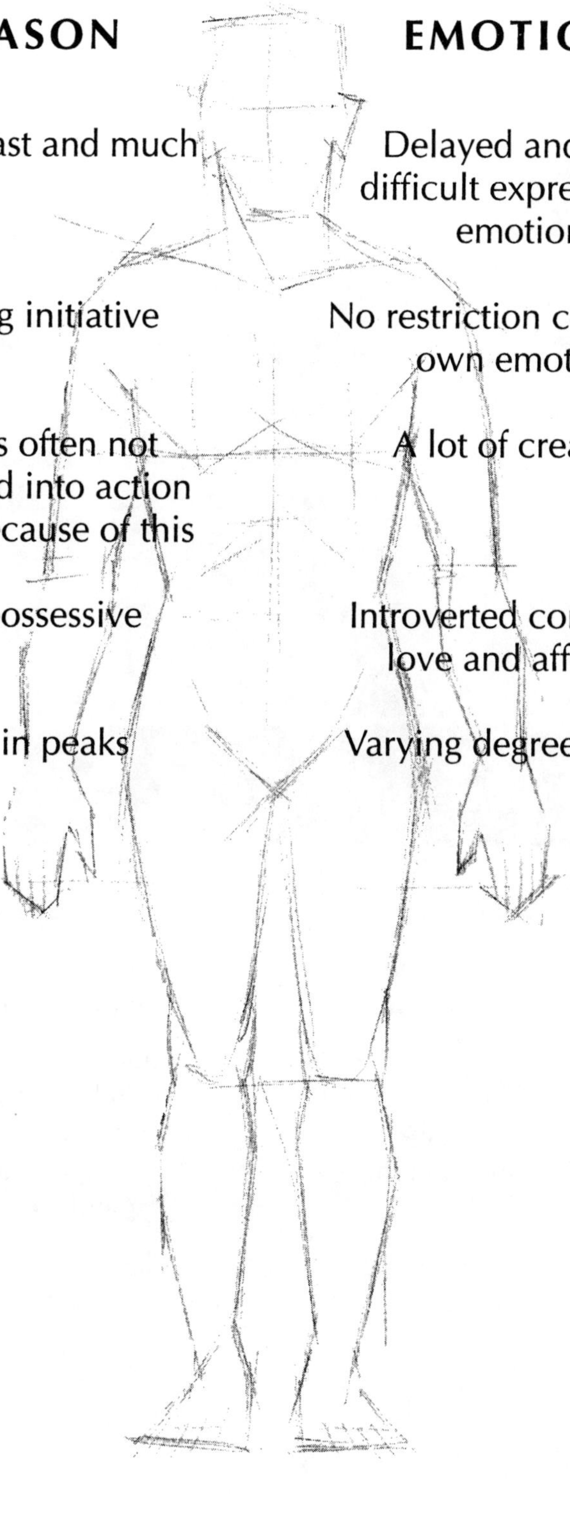

♀

CHARLOTTE

7 YEARS

Sophie – Female – 39 Years

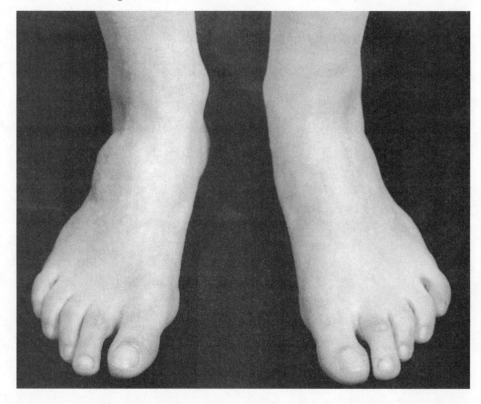

RIGHT	LEFT
Smaller ether-toe than on the left one Rush-toe Lump at the base Tip coming to an asymmetric point	Ether-toe with bottleneck coming to a point flattened tip
Slightly clawing wish-toe Callosity on first phalanx	Emotion-toe broad at base slightly narrowing Callosity on first phalanx Angular, almost spatula-shaped tip
Clawing, stiff activity-toe	Clawing creativity-toe Retro-toe
Strongly clawing attachment-toe	Clawing love-toe
Withdrawn, strongly clawing fear-toe	Pointy, active trust-toe with twist

Crooked toes are always found on the feet of people who are dominated and take it all lying down. With Sophie this is the case. She has learned to adapt in life, and she has adopted a behavioural pattern that wasn't originally hers. Either the outside world enforced adaptation, or she wanted to conform in order to go down well with others. The lumps at the base of her big toes indicate servitude. On the left foot is a smaller lump than the right one. Her servitude is therefore more rational and less emotional. Sophie does, however, know what she wants. Both her air-toes are reasonably straight, but when it comes to the realization of her desires, only a few of them are realized. From the broad outsides of her feet, but especially her left foot, we can derive that Sophie has a lot of earthly energy present in rudimentary form. Nothing much has come of its development. It got stuck in a reservoir.

♀

SOPHIE

39 YEARS

The right ether-toe tells us a story of suppressed self-expression. The ether is not very big and spacious. The tip comes to an asymmetric point. This is the ether-toe of someone who allows others to shut her up regularly. The asymmetric tip, which is inclined towards the wish-toe, shows us that occasionally, after some time has elapsed, Sophie can express what she wants rather fiercely. The gap between the wish-toe and the ether-toe tells us that expressing her wishes very vehemently on occasion only happens after some brooding. She stores up loads of anger and frustration until, suddenly, her feelings burst out. The first phalanx of the wish-toe is covered with some callosity. As soon as a desire develops she adopts a reserved attitude ("I won't say anything yet"). The toe is slightly bent towards the earth. Some of the wishes drain away almost completely unnoticed. The fire energy in the right foot has a hard time. The activity-toe bends towards the ground after the first phalanx. The toe can't be manipulated at all. Still the wish-toe and the activity-toe work closely together. Covertly, out of view, some of what Sophie wants is realized. Covertly, because the activity-toe hides from view a little. The attachment-toe also flushes energy down the drain. The tip rests flatly upon the ground, instead of pointing straight forward. So getting attached to something isn't allowed. Those around her don't approve and the attachment is therefore not worked out. These attachments are reasoned away and certainly not brought into the ether. She doesn't talk about it. The fear-toe claws in a similar way. The tip of the toe is entirely stashed away. So little of the originally offered energy is expressed, that even the little nail lacks energy to grow. It is exceptionally small and deformed. Fear and unease: don't talk about it and it won't be there.

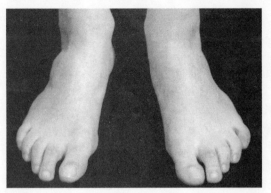

The left ether-toe develops after some hesitation (bottle-neck) and then comes to a point. Here is someone who hesitates to express her feelings. Nonetheless she decides deep down to do exactly that and throttles back, only to express a little part of her feelings in a rather bold way. That bold part is because the tip of this ether-toe is flattened. The energy is offered in a block shape. The tip of this toe hammers out a part of the emotions, as it were, yet the edges have been softened. Before the energy reflected in the emotion-toe is brought into the ether, a delaying detour is made. Because of the gap there is no direct contact between the emotions and the ether. After a lot of emotions have developed, they are immediately covered with a little callous layer, to prevent the outside world from seeing how much emotion there actually is. The toe tapers a little, but is straight and rather angular, almost spatula-shaped. She doesn't express her feelings in a sensitive way. If someone is trampled underfoot, or if other people's feelings are hurt, her attitude is: "I'm sorry, but it's your problem, not mine!" The creativity-toe is twisted towards the emotion-toe. This means: no creativity without feelings. However, nothing much comes of her creativity, because most of the energy is drained into the earth. You often see this pattern when creative, playful children keep being told: "Stop acting the fool, be your age, sit still and behave yourself for once!" The love-toe claws too. As soon as love starts flowing it branches off. The tip of the love-toe is in close contact with the ground. By draining love into the earth, Sophie will never be able to love wholeheartedly. The trust-toe is a toe with a lot of bottled-up energy: swollen and coming to a sharp point. The toe is twisted towards love, and touches the love-toe with its tip. All energy of which the trust-toe is a reflection is aimed at love. The elaboration of sexual feelings and instincts will only be possible if they work together with love. However, a change may be at hand concerning trust and sex. The toe is red and therefore displays increased activity.

♀

SOPHIE

39 YEARS

REASON   # EMOTIONS

Forced expressing and   Undiplomatic delayed
being silent   expressing

Imaginary desires   Displaying feelings
strongly

Restrained decisiveness   Undeveloped creativity

Ignoring attachment   Rejection of love

Denial of fear   Trust and sex dependent
on love in peaks

SOPHIE
39 YEARS

105

John – Male – 42 Years

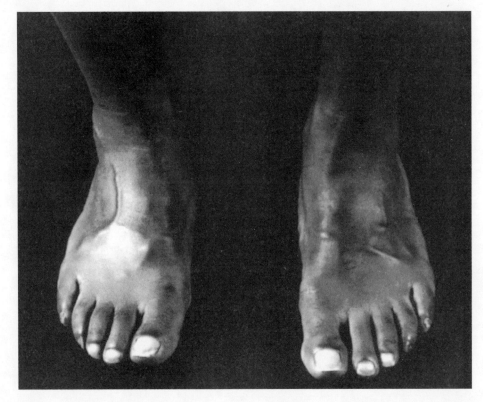

RIGHT	**LEFT**
Ether-toe with slight bottleneck angular tip round corners	Ether-toe with bottleneck angular tip upturned
Long, round wish-toe not earthed completely can be withdrawn	Block-shaped emotion-toe
Relatively large activity-toe slightly crooked with considerable drop (not visible in photograph)	Big, relatively bulky creativity-toe slightly crooked drop
Pointy attachment-toe, looking back with large drop	Backward-looking love-toe
Pointy, twisted fear-toe	Twisted, crooked trust-toe

106

John's trust-toe is pointy and twisted. This means that trust and sexuality come in waves. There are moments when John is so full of trust that he's sitting on top of the world without a care. He deals with his sexuality in the same fashion. The twist of the toe towards the love-toe indicates that sexuality without love is not even an interesting option.

John is noticeably more certain of his emotions than of his thoughts. His decisiveness is immediately apparent because of the big activity and creativity-toes. The three upper chakras show a well-balanced picture. The lower two are less balanced. John is obliging, but not so much as to let it be at his expense (small lumps on the sides of the big toes).

The horizontal ripple-marks on the nail of the right ether-toe which indicate a momentary lack of stability in the emotional field are not very visible. John can be hurt easily. The round tip indicates that John would rather choose a tactful approach than say things in plain terms. The slight twist indicates that John modifies his conversation to suit the listener. The toe is broad in the middle and then tapers off towards the tip, and this shows that John has more to say than he actually does. The inverse wedge shows that John has learned to express what he thinks more quickly. The wish-toe shows a lot of prominently present (angular tip) ambition. But because it does not touch the ground, it is not always easy to communicate his wishes and ambitions in plain language. The toe can be withdrawn, so John is able to adapt himself to his surroundings and present himself as a man with fewer ambitions than he actually has. But his true nature always surfaces quickly. The activity-toe is well-developed and has a considerable drop (not visible in photograph). The drop indicates that, just when you think John has reached the end of his tether, there is a reservoir of energy that enables him to go on for nights on end if necessary. This characteristic always pops up and surprises both John and the outside world. The slight bend shows that John has conformed in the past under pressure from those around him, and diverted part of his activities into the earth at his own expense. This pattern has changed, however, because the toe can be withdrawn, which does not cost him anything at all. The attachment-toe has a drop. This causes John to become fierce and furious if something is taken from him. Tact and friendliness are nowhere to be found when John is like this, but it only happens when he is robbed of his certainty. Aggression only comes to the surface when achievements are threatened. The pointy fear-toe shows that insecurity and fear come up in fierce, penetrating waves. The twist in the toe indicates that John does not like to talk about fear and insecurity. However, the base of the toe is straight. This means that

♂

JOHN

42 YEARS

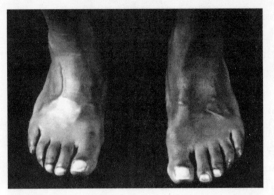

John can talk about said fear and insecurity — that is to say, about their origin, their foundation.

The left ether-toe has a stronger bottleneck than the right ether-toe. This means that there is more insecurity, more doubt, about expressing matters of the heart than those of the mind. After overcoming the hesitation, the emotions are eventually communicated, but more clearly and more emphatically than the product of his thoughts. This is derived from the angular shape. The inverse wedge between the ether-toe and the emotion-toe shows that John has learned to express his feelings more quickly and easily. The emotion-toe is long and spatula-shaped. The more John deals with his feelings, the stronger they become. His feelings snowball. The inverse wedge between the emotion-toe and creativity-toe indicates that it used to take some time before emotions were transformed into creativity, but that now it takes considerably less time. The creativity-toe has quite a drop. When John is being creative, he can carry on where others would normally stop. To the surprise of others and himself, he can mobilize unexpected amounts of decisiveness, when you would think that he has used up all his resources. The love-toe is equipped with lots of energy. When eventually love is set free, it can be overwhelming, even oppressive. But because the toe looks back John will be inclined to throw himself into creative matters wholeheartedly. He would rather do that than express his love in a physical way. The tip of the toe is under pressure. Love energy is active and ready for action.

JOHN

42 YEARS

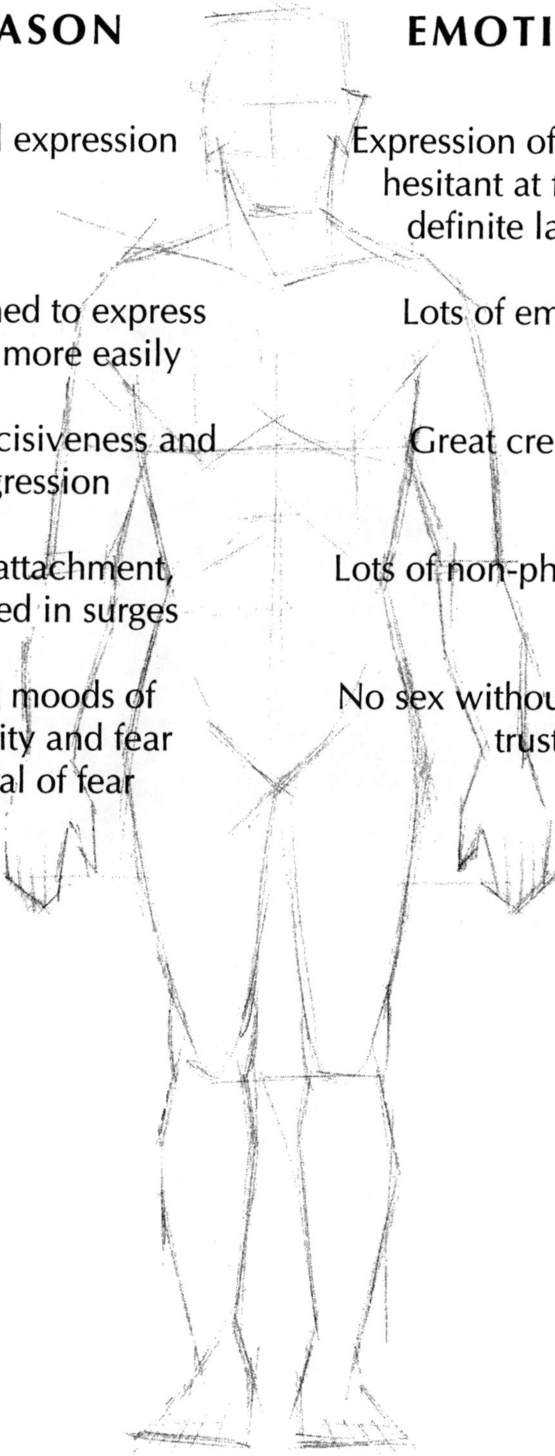

REASON

EMOTIONS

Tactical expression

Expression of emotions
hesitant at first, but
definite later on

Has learned to express
himself more easily

Lots of emotions

Lots of decisiveness and
aggression

Great creativity

Strong attachment,
expressed in surges

Lots of non-physical love

Strong moods of
insecurity and fear
Denial of fear

No sex without love and
trust

♂

JOHN

42 YEARS

109

Carolyn – Female – 36 Years

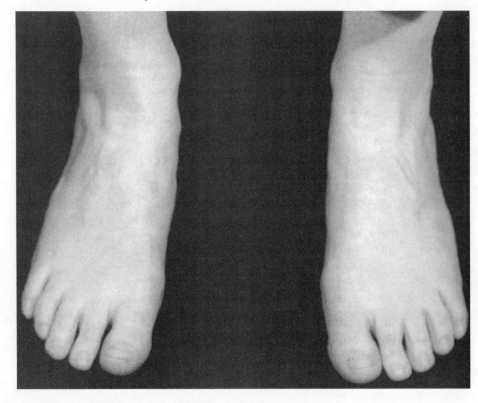

♀

CAROLYN

36 YEARS

RIGHT	**LEFT**
Ether-toe with bottleneck Doubt between round and angular shape	Ether-toe with bottleneck with rounder shape
Gap between ether-toe and adjoining toes	Broad-rooted emotion-toe with bottleneck
Well-developed, activity-toe	Straight, flexible creativity-toe with asymmetric tip
Twisted attachment-toe	Clawing love-toe
Pointy fear-toe	Pointy trust-toe with inclination towards adjoining toe

110

Big ripple-marks on the nails of both big toes tell us that Carolyn had to take a big emotional hurdle a number of weeks ago (when you know how fast Carolyn's nails grow you can determine when exactly). Furthermore, you can see that the left ether-toe is somewhat bigger at the base than the right one. Carolyn's emotions and her reason are not in balance. The emotions dominate the picture. The size of the left big toe in proportion to the right one tells us that there is quite a lot of sorrow in Carolyn's life.

The first phalanx of the right ether-toe shows a bottleneck. This means: doubt concerning expressing thoughts. Then the toe becomes broad at the joint (reservoir). Before Carolyn expresses herself, there has to be a lot of pressure. Then she vacillates between bluntness and tact: the toe hesitates between a spatula shape and a round one. With Carolyn it is very hard to predict if she is in a flexible mood and will behave in such a way that she doesn't hurt anyone, or if she will choose a blunt "you'll-just-have-to-take-me-the-way-I-am" approach. This ether-toe shows the image of someone who wants a lot, and will eventually end up in a hurry making sure she gets it. The last phalanx of this big ether-toe is asymmetric, and collects most energy towards the wish-toe. There is a gap between the big toe and the next. Everything happening in the wish-toe that has to be channelled towards the right ether-toe in order to be brought into the ether has to make a detour through the root of the ether-toe. This causes a delayed reaction as far as wishes and desires are concerned. Between the wish-toe and the activity-toe (where the realization of ideas has to take place) we also find a gap. When the ideas have to be made concrete by adding fire energy, a detour has to be made, just as in the ether-toe. In practice this means that Carolyn will brood for a while on what she wants. The activity-toe is a straight toe with a little asymmetry in the last phalanx directed at the wish-toe. The fact that the attachment-toe looks back reinforces this impression. The activity-toe is, relatively, the most developed toe on the right foot. Because of this, there is quite a lot of fire, a lot of aggression, contained in this toe. There is anger because she doesn't succeed in converting her thoughts into something concrete when she wants something.

Carolyn can never get going immediately (because of the gap). Yet the outburst of anger (the toe can be withdrawn) can be postponed for a while. That is why the outside world, when she demonstrates anger or irritation, can't put a finger on the cause. The attachment-toe looks back a long way. The last phalanx very clearly looks out for the activity-toe. When Carolyn does succeed in achieving something, fire (energy) immediately ensures that she holds on to what she attained. Whatever the reason, letting go of

♀

CAROLYN

36 YEARS

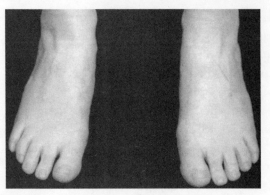

anything is very hard for Carolyn. The pointy shape of the last phalanx of the fear-toe reveals that fear rises very sharply sometimes. When Carolyn suffers one of her fits of fear, watch out, because these fits of fear are unrestrained, penetrant and deep-rooted. They can be held at bay for a long time. Carolyn doesn't hide from her fears. They are a nuisance, but she deals with them head on. Because there is direct contact between the earth energy, the water energy and the fire energy, it would be fair to assume that the fear is followed by anger.

The first phalanx of the left ether-toe has a bottleneck, just like the right one. Here too we have the initial doubt to express concerning, in this case, her feelings. The joint is broad also (reservoir). This toe is rounder than the big toe on the right foot. The emotions will be expressed in a softer way. Because the right ether-toe is a bit more angular-shaped, the rational expressions are presented a bit more boldly. The emotion-toe is very broad at the root. So initially there is a lot of energy present. After the start, the emotions flow into the bottleneck. Here it stagnates a bit. This causes inner unrest, because there are many more emotions than can actually be expressed. The tip of this toe is inclined towards the creativity-toe. A rush. The creativity-toe is straight, but its tip is slightly asymmetric and it is somewhat isolated. The creativity looks out for the emotions, as it were, and looks back. The tilt in this toe indicates too that the creativity falls back on the emotions, but also that it is inspired by the past (retro-toe). The toe is not in good, balanced contact with the emotion-toe. They touch eventually, but there is no constant contact during the creative processes. Carolyn doubts a lot, but she carries on. The last phalanx can be withdrawn very well. She can handle her creativity easily: "It's not that important." The love-toe points to the earth. A part of the love energy is or was flushed down the drain. The clawing position indicates frustration as far as love is concerned. The little toe, the trust-toe, comes to a point and its last phalanx points earthwards. This one is inclined towards the love-toe too. Sex without love will therefore be rare. The pointy tip of the toe tells us that sex is not one of her daily activities.

REASON

EMOTIONS

Variable way of
presenting thoughts

Emotions dominate and
are expressed dominantly

Expressing desires
after a delay

A lot of emotions
at the outset

Lots of fire i.e.
aggression

Creativity falls back
on past
Link to emotions

Strong attachment

Sex and love unity

Fits of fear in peaks

Varying degrees of trust

♀

CAROLYN

36 YEARS

Martha – Female – 30 Years

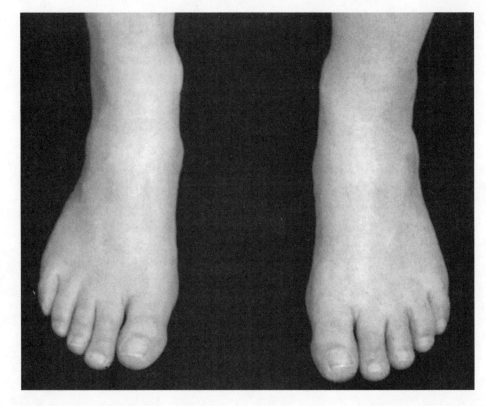

RIGHT	LEFT
Shorter ether-toe with reservoir Bottleneck Last phalanx a little pointy Round tip	Ether-toe with bottleneck, reservoir and round tip
Wish-toe with spatula shape	Flexible emotion-toe with rounded spatula shape
	Creativity-toe ending broader
Flexible activity-toe	Slightly clawing love-toe Slightly twisted last phalanx more flexible than at first glance
Attachment-toe partly hiding under activity-toe	
Twisted pointy fear-toe	Twisted pointy trust-toe

To "toe the line" of the energies of the other toes, the right ether-toe should have been an inch or so longer than it actually is. The left ether-toe appears to be a bit bigger than the right one. This indicates that Martha expresses her emotional life more easily, with more certainty, than her rational thoughts.

The right ether-toe shows us that Martha expects more from herself than is realistic. Her personal ether is too small for all the ideas that come bubbling up. As she talks, she will make a chaotic impression. This toe has a bottleneck. This means that Martha does not immediately express what she thinks. The big toe clearly broadens at the joint and forms a reservoir. Here Martha stores what she will say when she has overcome the hesitation of the bottleneck. Before she says anything, she "bottles it up". The last phalanx comes somewhat to a point, and is inclined towards the wish-toe. This deviation from its straight course tells us that Martha has a tendency to hurry, that she talks a lot and fast. She does, however, keep her cards close to her chest. The right big toe has a round tip, which means that Martha will try to avoid hurting people with her remarks under any circumstances. The most striking feature of the wish-toe is that its last phalanx is somewhat spatula-shaped, and that it is somewhat inclined towards the little toe. Martha is open about her material desires. The fact that the last phalanx is inclined towards the little toe indicates hurry and impatience. The spatula shape of this toe is in contradiction with the round shape of the ether-toe. This means that first she will naggingly harp on the same string for a while, and then, a little hesitantly, apologize. The activity-toe is straight, and has adapted to the shape of the right ether-toe. The wrinkle on the last joint indicates that 'doing' (aggression or action) can be temporarily postponed. The last phalanx clearly adjusts itself to the line of the other toes. It has an asymmetric tip. On the side of the wish-toe there is a lot of energy, on the side of the attachment-toe there is little. This means that at first, a lot of energy is put into all kinds of things, but when the results fail to materialize quickly, the zeal to persevere disappears. The attachment-toe appears to be straight. On closer inspection a big part of the toe turns out to be hiding under the activity-toe.

To the outside world, Martha appears to deal with attachment in a normal fashion. However, the shape of this attachment-toe reveals that Martha looks back, and she has difficulties detaching herself from material preoccupations. The little fear-toe is straight, but it has a strange twist. The part that should touch the ground looks out for the attachment-toe. The base doesn't touch the ground. Expressions of fear are therefore not founded.

♀

MARTHA

30 YEARS

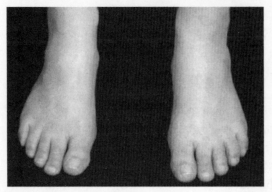

They can have their origins in the past or in the subconscious. The tip of this toe is pointy. The shape of this toe indicates fear rising in peaks.

The left ether-toe shows that the emotions are expressed in the same way as rational thoughts: hesitantly at first (bottleneck), then with a little more pressure (reservoir), and eventually with the edges blunted (round). The somewhat straighter shape of the last phalanx justifies the assumption that Martha deals with her emotions more easily than with her rational side. She is more sure of herself when she talks about emotional matters than when talking about the rational ones. This toe too is a bit short, but less clearly so than on the right foot. The emotions can be organized better than her reason. Furthermore, this ether-toe reveals the presence of a lot of feelings. The first phalanx looks out for the emotion-toe, as it were. If the toe grew straight from its root, there would be an enormous gap between this toe and the emotion-toe. In the past, Martha must therefore have expressed herself reluctantly. The ripple on the joint of the last phalanx shows that Martha is able to handle her feelings. The last phalanx first wants to become spatula-shaped as it were, but is rounded off after that. This means that her feelings will be expressed despite everything, but that she will show consideration for other people's feelings in the process. The creativity-toe is a rather straight toe with a narrow base and a broader tip. The conclusion we can draw from this is that there isn't a lot of creativity in the base, but that at a further remove (second and third phalanx), there is an influx (broadening) of creative energy. Because the shape of this toe abuts the emotion-toe, it is more than probable that the extra creativity produced is nourished from the emotions. The love-toe is a reservoir of unexpressed love. This toe can't be manipulated. The toe claws a bit, and this always means that the outside world has enforced restraint. The last phalanx of this toe looks back to the creativity-toe. The feelings of love seemed more intense in the past, better, despite all obstruction. On further inspection, the toe appears to be reasonably flexible. This means "toe at work". The trust-toe has a strange twist and is very pointy. A large part of this little toe is hidden under the love-toe, by the way. Expressing love and sexuality is not one of Martha's strong points. But sometimes there is a surge of optimism.

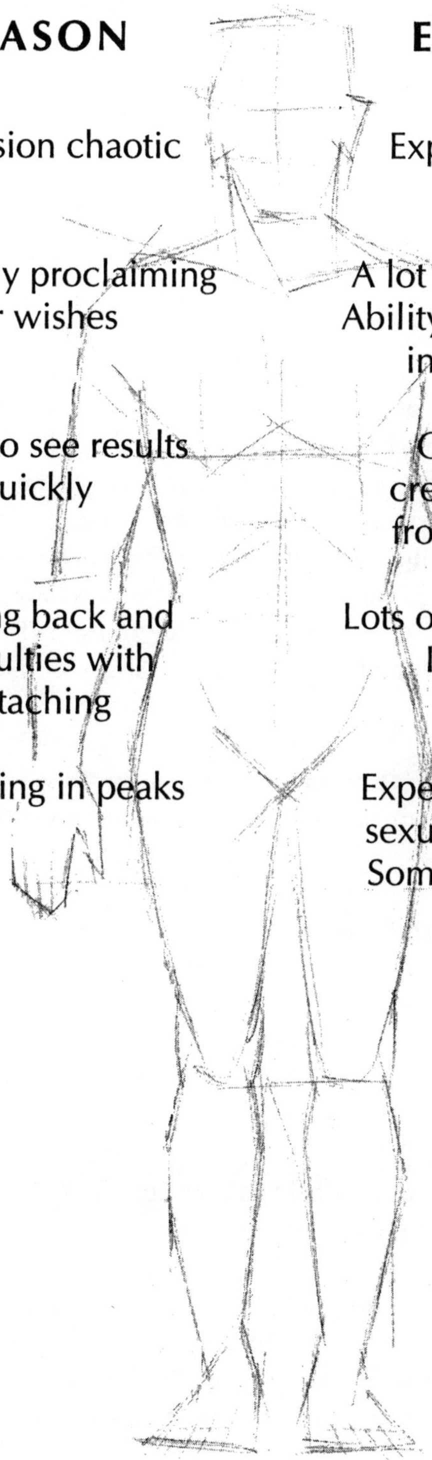

REASON

Expression chaotic

Constantly proclaiming
her wishes

Wants to see results
quickly

Looking back and
difficulties with
detaching

Fear rising in peaks

EMOTIONS

Expressing feelings
more easily

A lot of feelings present
Ability to deal with them
in a flexible way

Originally little
creativity, filled up
from the emotions

Lots of unexpressed love
Inner changes

Experiencing love and
sexuality less strongly
Sometimes optimistic

♀

MARTHA

30 YEARS

117

Comments

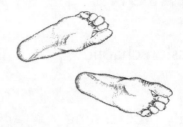

You will probably be curious to know how the owners of the toes from cases 1 to 17 have reacted to our analyses. We thought it necessary to record their reactions in this book, because there are people who feel the need to tell the whole story of their life after their toes have been read, or even while they're still being read. They forget that they have already done so by showing us their toes. Not everyone's comments have been printed, because two people couldn't or wouldn't say anything. Anyhow, you will get an impression of what kind of reactions you'll get in the future while practising toe-reading.

CASE 2. Peter: "Actually I do suffer from a lack of love. This occupies my mind a lot at the moment, and it probably explains my changing moods as well."

CASE 3. Hannah: "Yes, I do recognize a lot of the things you said. Well…some things I do not recognize…although, when I think about it, all of the things you said are true."

CASE 4. Matthew's mother: "It all ties in with his horoscope. I recognize a lot of the things you've said."

CASE 5. Henrietta: "It will probably all be right. I am out of a job, and I'm fed up with it. I definitely want to go to work."

CASE 6. Michael: "I do know what I want very well indeed, and I'm gradually managing to do more and more. But often things don't happen fast enough, and this does make me very angry. I recognize the bit about the creative process. I don't know about the fear, sex, optimism and trust part."

CASE 7. Sarah: "Strange that you can derive all that from the position of the toes. Everything is quite true."

CASE 8. Tony: "I believe the observations are quite correct...in fact, they are spot on. I am amazed."

CASE 9. Louisa: "It's true, I am searching for my identity, and I am in a state of flux. I just think that I need more than one life to figure it all out, but I'm trying very hard."

CASE 11. Jacqueline: "That delayed reaction bit is typical of me. I always react slowly, except after a massage. Apparently the energy flows so fast that I can express myself immediately and without restraint."

CASE 12. Leo: "Most of the things said are true, but they don't impress me. I think it's all a bit too general."

CASE 13. Charlotte's mother: "I am afraid that she is a victim of heredity. You're absolutely right about those fits of anger and aggression. When she doesn't get her way, she can get very angry. The thing about fantasizing is also true. She can play with her dolls and her cuddly toys in her own little dreamworld for hours, and act out complete plays. Don't try to pull her out of it, either, for she'll get angry again."

CASE 14. Sophie: "Most of the things you've said I can confirm immediately. About some of them I have to think a while before I agree with them."

CASE 15. John: "This is roughly correct. No, it is correct, period."

CASE 16. Carolyn: "I must say that I do recognize all of it. I would never have thought that my toes could tell so much about me."

CASE 17. Martha: "It is all reasonably true. What strikes me most is that the question of attachment comes up. I have been directing my attention more to women than men lately, and that suits me fine."

Postscript

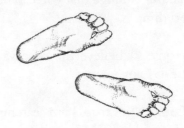

At lectures I have given about toe-reading, and in the introduction as well for that matter, I have stressed that toe-reading can be a most enjoyable party game. To get to know yourself and others better in familiar surroundings is always a good thing. Yet during my study and while putting my theory into practice, I became convinced that Reading Toes is more. It really is a method to analyze characters and to detect patterns of behaviour. I hope you don't have the impression that in this book everything has been said about this new phenomenon that there is to say. Far from it. We have confined ourselves to the outlines. We hope to have informed an audience as wide as possible, so that it knows what's going on when someone is "watching your toes" for a remarkably long time.

To be able to give guidance to the further development of this unique phenomenon, together with some others I have established a foundation, which should see to it that this development takes place in a responsible fashion. Of course I will also be a member of the executive committee of the foundation.

I would like to call on everyone who wants to respond to this book or wants to go into this method, or anyone with questions or suggestions, to get in touch with us. The name and address of the foundation are:

Stichting Fudare
(Foundation for Fundamental Dactylogical Reading)
P.O. Box 325
1200 AH HILVERSUM
The Netherlands
email: fudare@globalxs.nl
web-site: http://www.readingtoes.com